Introduction

Raising a teenager is a challenge that every parent has to be prepared to face. with the right information and parenting tactics. However, the parenting of a child begins with the values you instill in the child right from birth. This book contains an in-depth understanding on how you can raise your child appropriately to become a responsible adult with his or her own fair share of success.

The skills you will acquire from the book include how to help your teenage child through the different problems associated with teenage such as falling behind in academics, peer pressure, bullying, self-esteem, self-image, mental health problems, and addiction to the social media among others.

We appreciate your book choice and assure you it is a good one. A huge effort was put in the development of the content to make it as useful as possible in helping with your parenting problems.

Chapter 1: Relationship between Parents and Teens

Teenage is the age of a person as from 13 to 19 years. During this age/period, the person develops from the child he or she is into a mature person or adult. During this period, the child experiences many changes; starting from the brain. The limbic system and the frontal cortex parts of the brain undergo development that prepares the person for adult life. These changes affect the reasoning, behavior, and also the physical formation of the person. The change is mainly driven by hormones that are produced in the body. This change is so rapid that the parents are mostly left missing out on how their children reason and act. The behavior of an adolescent is also mostly influenced by the environmental aspects, society values, and norms. The body will release hormones, but the transformation of the person will, to a great extent, be influenced by societal expectations. It can be viewed in terms of the responsibilities accorded to people of a given gender by the society and the expectations in terms of relationships with people of different ages and the opposite sex. During this phase, the reasoning ability of the person progresses to adult level, and they can make logical decisions.

The Difficulties Faced by Adolescents in the Growth Period

The adolescent development stage occurs very fast. The biological changes take precedence over the psychosocial development, and with this, there arise conflicts in the child, parent, and society. The conflict is mostly based on the society's expectations, and the parents mostly find themselves at a loss on how to handle the transformed child. It is important to note that as the child develops into an adult, they still remain under the parental care and guidance, which might lead to some difficulties because their level of cognition and their bodies are already that of an adult.

Body Image and Self-esteem

A person's body image, especially in teenage, is highly related to their self-esteem. They both relate to how someone views themselves. The media has created the images of what a perfect look should be. Everyone has something they don't like about themselves, and if you place so much emphasis on the part of your body you find unattractive, you will end up hating it and spend a lot of time trying to change who you are. Parents are an important part of the formation of a child's body image and self-esteem. When parents say something negative about the body of their child, it affects how they view themselves. The parents need to focus on what's good about their children. If you keep boosting your child's confidence in their appearance from an early age, they will believe in the beauty of their body, and whatever negative comments their peers make about them might be categorized as malice. However, if a parent points out certain features about their children as being unattractive, the child will find difficulties in accepting their bodies.

How to Boost Your Child's Body Image

Teach your child how to accept their bodies. Let your child understand that no one is perfect, and everyone has their own insecurities when it comes to their bodies. Teach your child how to say positive things about themselves. This can be done by obviously pointing out what's beautiful about your child. Avoid making negative comments about your child's appearance.

Teach your child how to love their bodies. Loving the body goes hand in hand with treating it right. Encourage your child to eat healthily and exercise and let them know how important it is for their bodies to get the nutrients it needs. A child needs to understand how important their bodies are so that they can learn to appreciate it.

How to Boost Your Child's Self-esteem

Help your child learn how to do certain things that will boost the value they place on themselves. This can be how to play a certain sport, or dance, among others. Trying out new skills will help your child discover something they are really good at.

For a child with low self-esteem, associating with peers who treat him/her well would be quite helpful. If you find your child trying too hard to meet the standards of a certain group of peers, advice the child against it. Help your child understand the importance of hanging around people who love them for who they are but not having to change their appearance or things they love doing to be accepted.

Say positive things about your child. Avoid making negative comments about your child's appearance or abilities. Children take their parents' word for the gospel truth and whatever you say to your child about his or her appearance sticks in their memories for the longest time.

Teach your child how to accept the imperfections in themselves, especially the things they can't change. A parent should make their child understand that people were created different and unique. A parent can emphasize that their children are not any less but simply different and unique just like everyone else. If your child has a disability, try explaining to them that they are just special and not inferior in any way, and treat them so.

Help your child set some life goals and focus their minds today attaining them. Achieving set goals is very important in keeping a positive image of oneself. It keeps a person motivated and the more you achieve, the better you feel about yourself.

Train your child the importance of being helpful to others and giving what they have to help those in need. Giving gives a good feeling about self. The best way of doing this is by taking part with your child in charity exercises. You can even give your child something to take to someone who needs it more. This helps the child to feel useful and boosts how they view themselves.

Staying focused on the positive side of events is also a way of building up self-esteem. Avoid being negative all the time and teach your children to look at the positive side of things. When we stay negative, we attract negative feelings, and more things we do are more likely to go wrong. However, a positive attitude goes a long way in giving us the strength we need to stay focused on achieving good results.

The academic parent should also look at a child's effort to accomplish goals rather than how perfect they are in doing things. If your child is trying, let the child know that you are really proud of their efforts rather than criticizing them for not doing like you'd have wanted it done.

Academic Problems

Most children, at some point, fall back in their studies for various reasons. It is discouraging for a child to find themselves behind in class and, in some cases, children feel demoralized and end up dropping out of school. Others will simply stop trying to even understand whatever challenges them in classwork. There are several reasons why your child might be finding difficulties in academics, among them low attention span, your child might not be getting enough sleep at night, he or she might not be eating well, might also be due to lack of the required studying skills ,and the child might also be setting and focusing on the wrong priorities.

How to Help a Child Who is Falling Behind in Academics

A parent can involve the teacher of their child to establish the skills the child might be lacking in a particular class or topic. If your child missed on some foundational skills at a certain level, going upwards might prove problematic. Establishing the skills missing and bridging the gap will definitely help your child move forward in that particular class. You could employ the use of skill assessment to identify what the child might be missing.

Help your child identify and set out his priorities. A parent can set limits to entertainment and time the child spends with friends, on movies and television shows, or even playing video games.

Having limits to certain negative activities your child might be involved in, goes hand in hand with setting out certain times of the day when the child should solely focus on their academics. You can work with your child in coming up with a time table which indicates what times they should focus on which lesson in order to create balance. Some children might be focusing too much on the lessons they find interesting, and leaving those they find difficult.

A parent can help the child in acquiring certain skills that are basic in studying. A child might find themselves struggling with skills such as planning and taking of notes. With these skills, your child will feel more motivated to study.

Ensure your child gets enough sleep of 9 hours and has a consistent sleep pattern to avoid feelings of fatigue in class, which reduces concentration in most students. Ensure that your child goes to bed at a certain time and wakes up at a certain time. By doing so, the brain of the child is tuned to the sleeping pattern, and they will not find themselves sleeping during lessons.

Feed your children properly. With an empty stomach, the energy levels of a child go down, making concentration difficult. We should provide our children with a good breakfast with fruits and vegetables and enough energy to last them through the morning hours before they have their lunch. A healthy diet with enough fiber and limited fat content has been linked to children with high academic excellence.

Reading is one of the ways a child can increase their concentration levels. If your child has problems staying attentive in class, you can provide them with interesting books on the topics they love and encourage them to read them. You can come up with a certain way of motivating the child to read and most preferably, you could read together. The results will not be instant, but after a few weeks of reading for hours at a time, the attention span of the child will go up.

Difficulties Related to Family Problems

There are different family problems that teenagers have to overcome growing up. Every teenager has certain family-related struggles, which poses difficulties in their lives, causing stress and other times, depression.

Among these family-related problems are:

Parental Disagreements

Children, unknown to many parents, often get caught up between parental arguments. Wherever parents argue outside, it puts on a lot of stress on the children. Children always feel like they are responsible for the arguments especially if they revolve around money. This stress affects the well-being of the child psychologically. These arguments affect a child's academic performance, their social life, and makes them more withdrawn, and these children are more likely to turn out violent and break the law.

Children need to feel safe at home and protected by their parents. In a case where the parents are always in misunderstanding, the children are always insecure and on high alert, which leads to a lot of emotional stress.

Parents who are always in conflict with each other focus so much energy on their personal problems that they neglect the well-being of the children. Most of these children end up engaging in unacceptable behaviors and in a move to escape their problems; others engage in drugs.

Metal Illnesses of Parents/Alcoholics

Whatever dysfunctions a family goes through, the children are left clearing the mess for the rest of their lives. Mentally ill parents cannot provide for their children financially, emotionally, and not to mention giving the necessary psychological support they need. The children going through problems will not be able to handle them on their own, and most of them end up suffering psychological disorders.

The mental state of a parent is very important in raising children. A parent should seek help whenever they feel overwhelmed so that they can be emotionally capable of raising children. Mentally ill parents lack the capacity to raise children, with most of them mistreating them and others just neglecting their responsibilities to the children. Most children whose parents are suffering from mental health may suffer stigma from society and bullying from their peers. Parents should explain to their children about their illnesses and avoid lying about the details. This will make the children more understanding of their parent's situation and help them define ways of coping.

Alcohol, on the other hand, depletes family resources and results in financial constraints. Alcoholic parents are more likely to be abusive, negligent, and violent with the children. Children from families related to alcohol and substance abuse live in poverty. The strain from the limited resources leaves the children in a vicious cycle of poverty. The children from such backgrounds have limited chances of being successful. If a parent realizes that their alcohol intake is having a direct effect on the children, it's time to get help.

Financial Difficulties

Some parents raise their children in a loving environment despite their financial difficulties. Others are negligent of their responsibilities. The effect of the family's financial difficulties on a child all depends on the parenting technique. Parents who discuss their financial problems within the children's sight are more likely to affect their children feelings of safety. Such children will be thinking of financial problems and how they can help in making money for the family. Parents affect their children development. Other children carry heavy burdens which they cannot handle at their age; resulting in mental health-related problems. Even when a family is going through difficult financial times, parents should avoid involving their children in the matter. They should reassure their children they are fine and do what they can to give their children a comfortable life.

Teenage Mental Health-related Difficulties

One of the difficulties the adolescents experience is mental health problems. Serious monitoring of a child's behavior is very important. Research shows that 13 out of every 100 children of 8 to 15 years suffer from mental health illnesses, and half of these children go untreated. Every year in the united states, 1/5 children experience mental health problems annually, with 17 out of every hundred high school going children contemplating suicide. Half of the mental illnesses begin at 14 years old. Some behaviors children exhibit are related to some severe disorders which the earlier managed, the better. Children brought up in a violent and abusive environment are more likely to exhibit symptoms of more than one disorder.

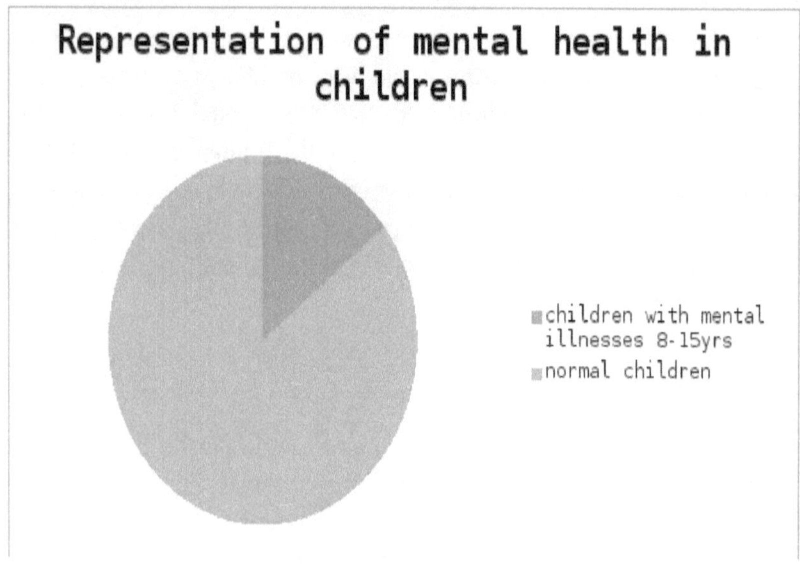

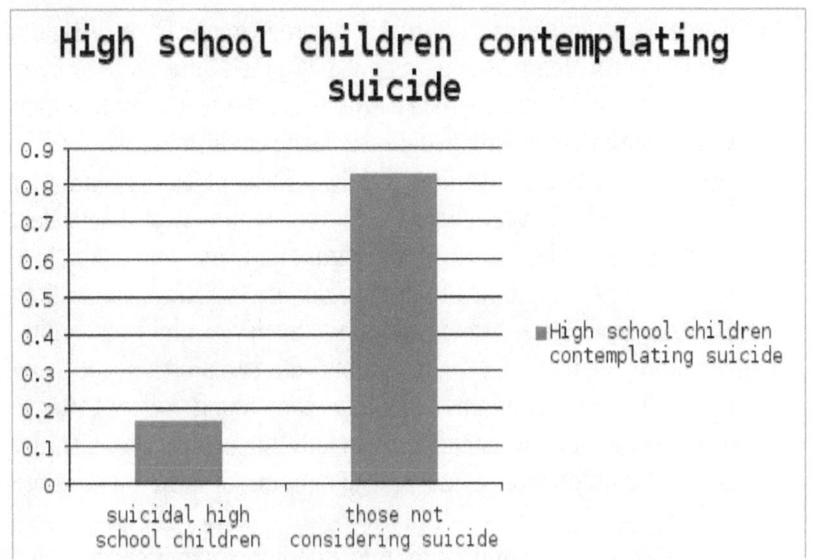

The common disorders among teens are:

Anxiety Disorder

Anxiety disorder is defined by worry and fear that affects the normal activities of a child. A health specialist can diagnose the condition, and proper medication and care can be given to help the child gain a normal functional life.

Anxiety disorder mostly starts showing in children and teens. One in ten children will have this condition, but as they grow up, most of them outgrow the anxiety; while in others, it progresses to adulthood where it becomes a serious problem. As the child grows up if proper clinical management is not put in place, the disorders culminate to depressive disorders.

Some of the childhood anxiety disorders include:

- Agoraphobia: this refers to the fear of being trapped in a dangerous place with no way out. This disorder is treated through behavioral therapy. In other cases, drugs may be administered but only to take care of the panic attacks, which might accompany the disorder. Some children with this disorder might have difficulty staying in crowded places or even leaving the house on their own. The fear the patients experience will affect the way they live their lives because they mostly avoid distressing environments.

- Generalized anxiety disorder: this is a form of anxiety disorder whereby the child experiences high levels of anxiety and persistent apprehension. The child goes through fears and excessive worrying. The symptoms of this disorder are sweating, exhaustion, somatic experiences, and tremors. Such a child is either hyperactive or restless or may exhibit both symptoms at the same time. Children with this problem are found to experience difficulties in staying attentive especially in school. This disorder can be a combination of several symptoms of different anxiety disorders.
- Panic disorder: a child with this condition experiences panic attacks which are more frequent and for less than 30 minutes. The children experience cognitive and somatic symptoms.
- Separation anxiety disorder: the child has a deep attachment to someone or an object, and in most cases, it is usually an attachment to the mother. The symptoms exhibited are closely related to avoiding the separation from taking place.
- Social anxiety disorder: This disorder is characterized by the child avoiding social places in fear of ridicule and embarrassment.

Specific phobic disorder: this disorder is characterized by an intense, unreasonable fear of certain situations or items. The child will try to avoid such objects. The cause of the phobia cannot be explained.

Stress-related Disorders

These are acute stress disorder abbreviated as ASD and posttraumatic stress disorder PTSD. These disorders occur when a child experiences or witnesses a stressful situation. The ASD condition is much shorter lasting up to one month, but if it is prolonged, it is then diagnosed as PTSD. In this case, children experience dreams related to the occurrence, recurring memories of the event, generally termed as intrusion symptoms.

Patients will try to avoid situations that remind them of the event.

People experiencing this disorder might have a distorted memory of the order of events of the particular experience, they may also exhibit a sense of guilt and shame as they feel responsible for what happened to them and they feel they could have avoided the occurrence from taking place. They may result in withdrawal from social life and lack foresight into the future.

It is also characterized by hyperarousal which exhibits in difficult in sleep, excessive aggression, inability to relax and pay attention; nightmares may also occur.

Dissociative related occurrences such as dissociation from the persons being and experiencing an unreal world.

The flashbacks for the occurrence are very dramatic and may cause a lot of distress to the child. The events seem to occur in real-time, and the child will get detached from the present. This is a serious medical condition that requires clinical evaluation. It is advisable to seek specialized treatment in time before the condition progresses. Clinicians find it easier to manage ASD as compared to PTSD.

Mood-related Disorders in Teens

This is a disorder that is followed by a loss and/or sometimes with the occurrence of a disappointing event. The child gets extremely sad and irritable. The mood-related disorders are:

- Dysthymia otherwise termed as Persistent depressive disorder: This mood of depression is mostly experienced for the most part of the day and almost every other day for a period of a year to two years. The symptoms of dysthymia are similar to those of major depression but are of lower intensity. The risk of major depression is very high, which can happen even before the end of the year set period for diagnosis. It will take the services of a specialist to diagnose and define this disorder based on the signs and symptoms.
- Major depressive disorder: this is characterized by a long episode of depression that can take up to a fortnight. 2 in every 100 children experience this. In adolescents, the number is 2 and a half times higher. If the person is not treated, a more severe depression might occur in less than a year. As the disorder checks in, the

person will be sad and teary for long periods. This will also be accompanied by irritable behavior. They will also lose interest in normal life activities that they used to enjoy being part of. Experiences of lack of sleep or too much sleep will be observed, low levels of appetite that will lead to weight loss, other people will notice psychomotor agitation unknown to the person experiencing them, the person will feel tired most of the time with low energy levels. Their levels of cognitions are affected with the adolescent's ability to reason, decision making, paying attention and logic quite affected, the person will think of committing suicide or experience fears of dying, they might also feel unworthy and blame themselves for it. This disorder is highly linked to drugs and substance abuse, and poor performance in school for a child who was once bright. Psychotic behaviors might also emerge when the disorder progresses.

- Disruptive mood dysregulation disorder: this disorder is characterized by changes in behavior that are quite extreme and uncontrollable. The person also gets constantly irritable. The disorder checks in from as early as six years. The earlier it is noted and diagnosed, the faster it can be contained. This disorder is in most cases accompanied by other disorders, and as the person grows past eighteen, anxiety might check-in. An adolescent with this disorder will experience irritable moods and anger that lasts for long hours and are quite significant to other people. They will also exhibit outbursts of temper that are extreme and inconsistent with their age: the episodes might occur several times per week. If not treated, the person might end up with a unipolar condition.

These depressive moods are accompanied by episodes of self-worthiness and suicidal thoughts in the adolescent. The moods come in variations whereby they are heightened by events that remind the person of the loss or disappointment they experienced. These negative feelings are accompanied by periods of more positive emotions and they occur interchanging. However, there is an improvement when the loss is reversed. In children, this disorder manifests in more of an irritable behavior rather than sadness. You will notice certain signs in the adolescent such as withdrawal from the social life they were once associated with; the person will show a drop in school performance and their actions are more aggressive. Mostly, they act in ways that are way out of their character and expectations.

Obsessive-Compulsive Disorder in Adolescents (OCD)

The individual with this disorder is highly obsessed with ideas and items, and this extreme obsession will lead them to act on impulse in pursuit of the items of obsession. If the impulse is restricted, the adolescent ends up behaving out of control. While the disorder starts from as early as fourteen years, the diagnosis can only be made at the age of nineteen.

There are several categories of this disorder:

- Body dysmorphic disorder: this is characterized by a person being too preoccupied with their looks that it is significant enough for the people they relate with to notice oblivious to the person experiencing it. The adolescent will have feelings of deformity, and they are constantly comparing themselves with other people. The treatment used in psychotherapy and some drugs may be subscribed. This problem is more associated with women, and two in every hundred people will experience it in their lifetime. The concern with appearance may vary from one part of the body to the other, and the condition is rather serious if not treated. It affects the ability of the adolescent to socialize and take part in events that may greatly affect their academics. The levels of obsessions vary. While some people with this disorder are constantly drawn to mirrors, others will avoid them. The person will have feelings of inadequacy based on their perceived malformation, thinking that other people are noticing it. They feel like the peers, and the people they associate with will be judging them based on the appearance of the body parts, and most of them result in excessive makeup, constant picking on pimples, cosmetic surgery which ends up increasing on their insecurities. In most cases, men will have muscle dysmorphia, which leads them to use androgen hormones to boost their appearances. Some people in extreme cases will only leave their homes at night to avoid being seen, they will avoid going to school and being in other social places. This disorder is associated with cases of suicide. This disorder is always related to poor academic performances.

- Hoarding Disorder: this is attributed to the attachment to items of less significant values that leads to the cluttering of the living environment to the point of excessive congestion and difficulties in normal functioning. The adolescent will find it extremely difficult to let go or throw away items. Up to 6 in every hundred people will experience the hoarding disorder. This condition begins at teenage, and if not treated, it worsens with age. The living places of the persons with this disorder are transformed into hoarding places distracting the norm. This disorder is associated with the person falling out on social life as they will find difficulty in allowing people into their homes due to the shame associated with the clutter they are hoarding. In other cases, people with the disorder have increased attachment to animals whereby they have an excess animal which they are not able to take good care of in term of health and food. These animals cause filth within the living spaces which the person gets accustomed to living with. While some people may take note of their disorder and seek help, others remain oblivious to it.

- Trichotillomania: this is an obsessive-compulsive disorder that leads to pulling and plucking of hairs causing balding. The hair may be plucked off different body parts, and this comes with a sensation of relief from anxiety and tension they might be experiencing. 9 in every ten people experiencing this disorder are women, and the problems start at teenage progressing to adulthood. The person will take note of the disorder and try to control themselves, but it might prove impossible without the help of a specialist. The patterns of hair pulling in a person are consistent in that the person will pluck it in a certain direction, and some people chew on it and swallow leading to another health-related problem termed as trichobezoars. This is a digestive problem associated with loads of hair that the body is unable to get rid of and they are removed surgically. This behavior is also a cause of embarrassment to the person and they will attempt to hide it. In other rare occasions, patients with this condition develop a habit of pulling animal fur, pulling hair from other people and wool/strings from clothing materials.

- Excoriation/ Skin picking disorder: this is a disorder that might also occur in teens. People with this disorder have lesions on their body with outer skin missing. A huge fraction of people who experience this disorder are women. However, two in every hundred people will have the disorder at least once in their lifetime. Some of the patients will scratch and pick on some spots or pimples on their skin because they don't like them while others will go for the healthy skin as an obsessive behavior when they are subjected to events of anxiety and stressful situations. In this case, skin picking gives them a sense of satisfaction and peace. The act of picking the skin leads to feelings of shame to the person, and they will do excessive makeup and the type of clothes that will hide the damaged skin. In severe cases, the patients will experience consequential health problems such as septicemia, bleeding, and skin infections. Other disorders usually accompany this disorder. Patients will try to stop themselves, but they experience anxiety whenever they try not to pick on their skin.

Disruptive Behavioral Disorders

This refers to a wider range of behavior related disorders. They are:

- Oppositional defiant disorder: This is an attitude of defiance towards figures of authority.
- Conduct disorder: this disorder is mainly associated with violation of the societal expectations, breaking of the law included.
- Hyperactivity disorder/attention deficit disorder otherwise abbreviated as ADHD: this condition is classified under neurodevelopmental disorder because it starts developing in a child from quite an early age (before preschool). The condition occurs in 3 types: predominantly hyperactive and impulsive, predominantly inattentive and thirdly we have cases where both of these conditions are combined. The experience difficulties in social life, problem-solving, language, perception, memory, and attention. This disorder affects up to 11 in every 100 children, and it is one of the most misdiagnosed disorders. The causes are behavior-related factors, physiologic, sensorimotor, biochemical and genetic related factors. Some risk factors are related to the disorder, and they include prenatal exposure to drugs and

substance abuse (cocaine, tobacco, and alcohol), obstructive sleep apnea, iron deficiency, head trauma, and children born underweight (below 1.5kgs).

Behavioral Difficulties

Adolescence is a stage of transformation to adulthood, and parents need to recognize that the child they are raising is being prepared to become an adult--a process that is beyond their control. The process is rather difficult for the teenager because they are already equipped with the abilities to make decisions, but at the same time, they feel they should comply with their parents who are their source of security. This process is signified by most adolescents' changes in behavior as they divert from the rules set out by their parents. The nature of parenting should adjust to adapt to the changes taking place in the child. It, therefore, calls for understanding between them and the side of the parents. At this age, the transformation is very rampant, and the adolescents will want to rediscover the newfound self. This leads to behavior that is related to adventure. They are also developing independent cognitive and decision-making abilities, and as a result, they will feel like they are mature enough to make life-changing choices. These factors lead to behaviors such as

- Drugs and substance abuse: Most people who are addicted to drugs started at teenage. There are various reasons for the use of drugs by adolescents. Mostly it's the peer pressure from their agemates and schoolmates as they try to fit in. The need to fit in is so much is experienced by teenagers as they are not yet fully aware of themselves. The use of drugs at that age is seen as cool, and if you are not into it as a teenager, you will feel left out and are bound to be discriminated.

Teenagers tend to form groups that they feel most comfortable in. These groups are composed of peers wuthering similar experiences, and due to the level of importance the teen attributes to these social cliques, they will divert the time they once spend with family and shift it to their peers. They rely on each other for advice, decision-making, and many other forms of social support. In these groups, behaviors they see at their homes such as drugs and violence are shared.

Researchers have found out that adolescents are drawn to peers with similar behavior as those of their parents or those advocated by parents. It has also been revealed that the habits of teens to be drawn to peers is born from their common experiences in terms of their bodies.

- Incidents of violence and harm: The explorative nature of a teenage might result in them causing harm to themselves. They feel the need to experience extremes of life, and thus, they are more likely to find themselves in an accident and engaging in fights.
- Sexual adventures and experimentation: With their developed bodies and high hormone levels, teenagers a more likely to be lured into sex than any other age bracket. Peer pressure is also a contributing factor to these sexual acts. Due to their inexperience in sex, they are at a higher risk of getting exposed to sexually transmitted diseases and unplanned pregnancies.
- Risky illegal acts: This is the breaking of the law among teens.

How to deal with rebellion in teenagers

A parent will notice a child's rebellion from their persistent behaviors. A child may start talking back at you, dropping out of class, and constantly getting themselves in trouble. A child showing these signs will need to be looked at keenly before they move from worse to worst. Rebellion in teens is about a state of adventure as some try to see how far they can go by doing the extreme.

When your child is rebelling, it is normal for a parent to establish strict rules on the child as a way of controlling them and disciplining them. However, avoid being too strict as we have seen a teenager in rebellion is trying the extreme. Being too strict will be like you are challenging them and they will go for it. It is advisable to relax a bit on your strictness and let your child adjust to that space.

It is also important not to give in and let the child disobey you. Whenever you instruct your child to do something, it should be done. The child should know that you are firm on your decisions.

Try reasoning with your child to see the sense behind their actions.

Sometimes, children are trying to avoid certain outcomes that the parent is not ready to listen. If you listen to the views of your child, you might find it reasonable. You can tell the child to give you time to think about the situation if need be. However, don't be hesitant to give in if you find your child's actions reasonable.

Your children need space. Giving your children their private space will not prevent them from lying and hiding things. Most importantly, let your child know that you respect their space, but they should be open with you.

Let your children understand your rules so that they don't give excuses for breaking them. You should also tell them why you require things done in a certain way so that they can give their feelings on it to avoid conflict in the future.

Finally, it's important to let your child learn from experience. If your child is in trouble in school or outside, let the child face up to the consequences of their actions. Most teenagers find breaking rules fun when they know their parents will stand up for them. However, if your child knows there is no way of evading the consequences, they will not be so eager to be on the wrong side.

Guidelines on Disciplining your Child

The logic behind discipline is learning to act appropriately, not punishment. Unlike children, teenagers are disciplined in ways that will help them learn how to solve problems, act responsibly and also learn to be independent. When you are trying to teach your teenage child, you work together in defining the limits to their actions with the logic behind it. As you set the limits, you also come up with the consequences of going contrary to the said rules.

Discipline is most effective when the parents are loving and warm towards their children. With that in mind, it is important to talk through with your child regarding what's appropriate and what's not in terms of their actions. You can define boundaries on behavior by discussing your expectations with your child and why it is important in terms of having a successful future. Since the boundaries are agreed on, a parent should be ready to adjust if need be.

When working on your child's discipline, it is important to acknowledge their good behavior and reward. This is a way of motivating your child to act appropriately. Failure to acknowledge the good things that your child does creates a negative attitude towards your rules and make them feel like they are constantly being reprimanded or are not able to satisfy your demands no matter what they do.

Involve your child in defining the consequences of inappropriate behavior. The consequences must be linked directly to the act. For instance, if your child leaves their rooms untidy, you can have them do their own cleaning as a way of learning so that as they clean, they can think about their actions. If your child acts contrary to your agreed rules, you can stop cooperating with the child as a way of reinforcing behavior. For instance, in the above example, you could withdrawal the cleaning services and let everyone do their own cleaning. You can also do so by taking away some of the privileges your child enjoys. Before you apply the consequences, let your child know what he or she did wrong and what you both agreed as the consequences to the behavior. Always be consistent with the consequences you agree on so that your child can take the process seriously.

The Changes that are Likely to Occur in the Relationship between the Parents and the Child at Adolescence

As a person navigates through the childhood stage to adulthood, the relationship with their parents also changes for several reasons. There is a reduced communication between the parent and the teenager, which brings in a gap and results in conflict and perceived hostility grows. At this stage of life, the teen needs the guidance of the parents despite their dire need for independence. The relationship between the child and the parent solely depends on the roles the parents play in the child's lives and their parenting techniques. The responsibility of the parents changes as a child moves to adulthood as follows:

The parents will need to change their parenting techniques. They change their roles from making decisions for the child to helping their children make their own decision through advice and guidance to avoid endangering their lives.

A parent still remains responsible for educational support and shaping the future of their children. Parents are responsible for giving the required guidance on the cultivation of positive values in their teenage children. The parents need to give the necessary advice and let their teenage children understand the consequences of their behavior in the formation of their future.

The development and cultivation of healthy relationships by teens with their parents help the children in acquiring positive behavior such as abstaining from drugs, alcohol, and sex. However, the negative relationship between parents and their teenage children result in pushing their children to negative psychological behaviors that mostly lead to drugs, violence, substance abuse, and unsafe sex that might result in sexually transmitted diseases and teen pregnancies. The development of healthy relationships will also give the child a healthy psychological state of mind, such as self-esteem and happier life free from teenage related psychological disorders.

Different Parenting Techniques

- Neglectful or uninvolved parenting technique: the parents, in this case, have trouble meeting the needs of their children, and thus, a healthy relationship involving with effective communication between them and their teenage children is rather difficult to establish.
- Indulgent or otherwise known as Permissive Parenting: These are the type of parenting techniques that offer little regulation of their children behavior, they have no laid-out expectations of their children's future, and they give in too easily to their children demands. These parents are very unstructured in their way of parkland they find it quite a challenge to control their children once they get to teenage.
- Authoritarian Parenting: this is a form of parenting where the parents have structured expectations of their children while offering limited support to achieve such and low levels of communication between the parents and their teenage children.
- Authoritative Parenting: In this parenting technique, the communication between the parent and the child is very healthy.

This parenting technique is defined by the parents having a set-out expectation of the future of their children while at the same time offering the necessary support they need to prosper in life. This is the healthiest and recommended parenting technique. It will give rise to responsible children who are less likely to indulge in drugs and other irresponsible behaviors. This parenting calls for strong communication techniques and strictly set out boundaries of the limits of a child behavior with defined consequences for inappropriate actions. Regardless of the background of any family, the parents are able to achieve this parenting technique in raising their children. This also applies to single parents and those of low financial backgrounds.

In parenting, the maintenance of an open communication environment is very important. According to research, teenagers are capable of communicating effects timely and openly with their parents if they know they will be listened to. The smooth communication between parents and teenagers gives rise to a healthy life to the adolescent as they are less likely to engage in immoral and unacceptable behaviors. Children in early teenage have challenges in expressing their needs to their parents.

Guidelines to Improve the Communication between Parents and Teenagers

- *When it comes to sensitive topics, talk early enough and in time*

This is in relation to matters of sex and drugs/substance abuse. There are so many sources of information in the media and peers. Delay in having these conversations will lead to alternative sources of information which might be misleading to the child.

- *Avoid being reactive*

Even when your teenage child is acting inappropriately, try not to show emotions, rather stay calm as you try to make them understand the consequences of their behaviors.

- *Ask questions that allow for the intensive supply of information*

If your child is telling you about his or her future plans, try to ask questions that will make them think through their decisions. As they outline their reasons for such plans, they will learn how to weigh the pros and cons of the decision-making processes.

- *Be an active listener whenever you are having a conversation with your teenage child*

Whenever your child is in a talking mood, try to listen more. Don't interrupt their speech, and whenever they ask for your opinion, try sharing with them your similar experiences as a teenager. This will create a more relaxed mood opening up a sharing session. Try by all means to avoid lecturing the teenager.

- *Provide your child with time to listen to him or her*

A parent should be able to create talking opportunities by engaging in activities of interest to the child; where they can engage in open conversations. Talking to them about topics they find interesting will make them more comfortable to open up. Whenever they start opening up, you should also be ready to listen and participate in the conversation actively.

- *Be supportive and provide a warm attitude*

Parents should be kind and supportive to their children, letting them understated they love them regardless of the circumstances. Children need to feel that their parents are there for them at all times and they can always go to them with troubles to seek assistance.

Tips that will help in keeping a close relationship with teenagers

- Take meals as a family and use this as an opportunity to talk about the day's experiences and achievements. Avoid the use of phones during meals.
- Engage in family events where you go out and have fun as a family. You can engage in events that can bond and encourage sharing, for example, sports and mind games.
- Look for opportunities where you can have a one on one conversation with your child. This can be at home as you do duties together, for example, cleaning the dishes. Encourage the child to share her daily experiences and friends. This way, you get to learn your child more. You can also share your own related experiences that creates trust.
- Whenever your child achieves something, take this as an opportunity to celebrate. Hold a family party and make it as much enjoyable as possible. Involve every member of the family in planning the party.
- Establish strong family practices and traditions that will keep the family together. Shared traditions will always bring the family together through shared values and making of memories we can go over and over through the years.
- Make use of the family rules to create consistency and stability for the family. Children love and thrive in a predictable environment, and uncertainty creates a sense of insecurity in the mind of children.
- Hold regular family meetings with set agendas and use them as a basis of solving issues and conflicts that might have occurred.

You can also make use of external support services such as counseling if you are unable to bring your family close. It is in the dream of everyone to have a concrete family. If your family is so much disintegrated, then there must be some underlying issues that might need the use of professional services to address them. If need be, don't hesitate.

Handling of Conflicts between Parents and Teenagers

As your child grows into a teenager, the occurrence of conflicts increases. This results due to their developing ability to make decisions. However, as a parent, it is your responsibility to handle the conflicts that occur and prevent it from escalating. Conflict is healthy in growing your relationship with your child, but it might be damaging if not properly managed.

It is important to stay calm about the situation and let your child know that you can only talk when he or she is calm. Be firm and avoid getting too emotional; if you find it hard, just take a break and let the child know you will revisit the issue later. Conflicts in teenagers can grow into fights if you fuel the fire. If the child results in violence and damaging of property stay calm, let the child know that there will be consequences for their actions and let him know that issue will only be handled when the child is calm. As they calm down, they will have an opportunity to think through their behavior. However, don't act in fear or show the child you are afraid of him or her as this will give them the power to harm you.

When you are both calm, allow your child to talk uninterrupted. Listen and control your emotions as you do so. Be warm and patient as you hear them through and ask appropriate open questions that will get them thinking through the issue at hand. Let the child talk through his or her emotions as you listen.

Maintain your levels of respect with your child as you talk and avoid talking back at each other. After hearing your child out, point out the mistakes they made. Talk about the current issue and avoid going over other issues in the past that might relate to what you are dealing with. You should also stay focused and shorten your statements. Let the child understand what's wrong about their actions. If as a parent, you realize that you made a mistake, be the first one to apologize about it. However, don't be moved to agreeing to inappropriate behavior.

Work out a solution to the problems that's acceptable to all parties involved. At finding a solution, you should be ready to negotiate with your child and teach him or her how to compromise in tough situations so that you can move forward. This solution must involve some consequences for the behavior of your child. Let the child understand that every action has consequences, and they must be ready to face the outcome of their behavior. Let the child understand how their actions affected you and other people, as this will teach them how to empathize with people they interact.

Smartphones teenage parent relationship

The smartphone technology has led to as many as half of the teenagers getting addicted to their phones. They find it difficult to let go of their phones, and this has immensely affected their communication skills at home. Unfortunately, the parents too find it difficult to put down their phones and engage in a traditional face to face communication with their children. However, all is not lost yet, as there are certain ways which a parent can use to help their teenage children overcome the addiction arising from the use of smartphones. When well used, smartphones can be quite healthy for an adolescent. The teenager needs to learn how to control their own use of smartphones without getting addicted:

It is important for the parent to take note of and monitor their own cell phone behaviors and set up an example for their children through role modeling. The children will accord more value to the set-out guidelines if they feel their parents are following the same strict rules they set out for them.

As a parent, you can strictly formulate some phone-free moments as a family where you can indulge in normal conversations. You can establish certain times, such as dinner time, family outings, where a person is not allowed to touch their phones. The parent should set an example by participation.

The creation of a check-in and check-out policy could be helpful. This refers to setting rules that do not allow the carrying of the cell phone to the bedroom at night when someone goes to sleep as they lead to cases of insomnia.

Use the existing technology to limit the use of cell phones. You can use tracking applications to monitor and set limits to the amount of time a teenage spend on certain sites such as social media. Most addictions arise from social media. While doing this, ensure that your child understands why it is important to have limits on the number of hours we spend on our phones.

As a family, you should come up with a plan on the boundaries of using the cell phone, and that's inclusive of the consequences of breaking the set-out rules. This also applies to the parents equally as any other member of the family.

Have an educative conversation surrounding the healthy use of a smartphone. A conversational context works best in correcting the negative behaviors in teenagers. During this conversation, you should make the child understand why it is unhealthy to stay glued to your smartphone, how such behavior affects every other aspect of your life such as academics and ability to have a healthy social life away from the social media.

Signs of Addiction to Social Media

- The person is very uncomfortable if denied the use of the phone.
- If the phone is not accessible the person experiences anxiety and irritable behavior.
- The person feels an urgent need to check out and reply to messages on their phones.
- In cases where the use of smartphones gives the individual a feeling of satisfaction or gratification.
- Behavior related to often checking their phones, which might induce insomnia.
- Inability to control the use of a smartphone to the point, it results in a major misunderstanding between family and friends.
- Constant inability to function properly at school and home attributed to smartphones.

What Parents Fear Most concerning their Teenage Children

Most fears parents experience is related to the possible failure as a parent in bringing up a responsible and dependable adult. However, the teenage stage of growth is very risky because the children are in the experimental and error phase of life. Teenagers engage in risky behaviors that are worrying to any parent such as:

- The fear of a child getting physically harmed from over-speeding when driving.
- Substance abuse and alcoholism are rampant at this stage.
- Teen pregnancies and sexually transmitted diseases resulting from premature sex and reckless sex behaviors.
- A child dropping out of school or academic poor performances due to peer pressure and irresponsible decision making.
- Sexual molestation and abuse.
- Fear related to addictions and psychological disorders.

Chapter 2: Motivation and Empathy

As a child goes into the teenage stage of development, they get rather too self-conscious, which can be translated to mean selfishness and completely lacking empathy. However, a parent can take up the responsibility of creating empathy in the child. Research has revealed that affective and cognitive empathy is still underdeveloped during the teenage years and due to this, teenagers might experience challenges in diverting their attention away from themselves to others. Cognitive ability is defined as the ability to reason and see things from another person's point of view. Affective empathy is defined as the ability to take notice of how other people feel and act accordingly. There are several ways through which you can promote empathy in a teenager.

How to Create Empathy in a Teenager

Empathy refers to the ability of a person to take note of the feelings of other people and put it into consideration by acting appropriately. Healthy levels of empathy will increase the chances of a teenage having a successful social life, academic prosperity and healthy relationships with parents and other siblings. A person develops empathy as from ages of 21; however, there are several ways to cultivate empathy in a teenager.

You can spark your teenage child to reason in matters of empathy, such as issues arising from watching news stories. You will achieve this by prompting the teenager to reason in lines of what is socially acceptable. Asking their opinions on different matters and actions of persons and their own opinions on how such matters can be handled.

Talk to the teenage about work-life and college life from your own experiences in relation to empathy. You can open up the teen's mind on how life can be difficult in areas of social life if a person is incapable of empathizing with the feelings of others. You can train the teenager to learn how to handle different personalities of people who contributed to a great extent their levels of prosperity in their career. These can be their colleagues at work and their bosses.

Certain life skills are also important in building a successful life with empathy. You need to train your adolescents on matters of:

- *Innovative thinking:* this refers to critical decision-making processes where people's feelings are at stake. The teenage child will benefit from skills related to problem solving and resolution of disputes and this will help the teenager navigate easily through social life in college and at work.
- *Leadership:* This refers to a teenager with certain responsibilities demanding for leaderships skills, you can give them some management tasks at a certain job and also give them certain home duties that demand planning. It is important for a leader to exhibit skills in empathy in order to be able to associate properly with people. Leadership comes with a lot of emotions from people whom the person works with. By inculcating leadership qualities in a teenager will enable the person to view the world from a different perspective. For instance, the adolescent will be able to learn how to deal with emotional situations.
- *Responsible actions:* A teenager should be able to take up responsibility for their actions. Whenever your teenage child does something contrary to the parent's set out expectations, appropriate punishment must come to play along with the correction of the errors and damage that might have occurred from the teen's actions. Teaching your child to take up responsibility for their actions trains them how to act with critical considerations of the outcomes of their behavior. Parents who fail to train their children to take up responsibilities for their actions end up experiencing difficulties in controlling them. They develop a sense of entitlement, and mostly they are inconsiderate of the feelings of their parents and everyone else.
- *Development of healthy relationships between parents and teenage children:* Research has shown that teens who have close and healthy relationships with their parents have a more likelihood of expressing empathy with other people. A parent needs to give a child a sense of security that will assure them of the parents' unconditional love and support. When a teenager's emotional, physical and financial needs are met, the child will express less distress with the parents and peers. Treat your teenage child as an individual with his or her own mind with the ability to reason and make decisions. This is mean that you cannot make decisions for a

teenager rather than simply helping them make a decision through reasoning through with them.

Handle your child as the unique being they are. It is aggravating for a teenager when you keep comparing him or her to yourself and other teenagers. This lowers their self-esteem. It is therefore important to understand your child and reason with them on behaviors you find unacceptable. Make them understand why certain behaviors would damage their life. Avoid using an accusing tone when trying to correct their actions because whenever accused teens start building up a defense that may be in the form of retaliation.

Motivation in a Teenager

Motivation refers to the pursuit of a motive. The motive demands fulfillment. The reason why most youths engage in some behavior can be looked at as originating from poor motivation to build a bright future for themselves by engaging in productive activities. The children who mostly engage in alcohol, sex, and drug abuse are looking for some way to feel alive. They lack focus and the ability to concentrate on useful activities. A teen without motivation might find boredom and monotony in normal daily activities such as eating, taking a bath and schooling. These could be assessed for the possibility of depression in that person.

We are going to assess the teenage lack of motivation from the Dr, Maslow's theory of the hierarchy of needs. According to this famous theory, a person will be motivated by the desire to meet their needs, and once the needs are met, the person then moves to the next level of needs. Every human being lives for a purpose to fulfill certain needs they find missing in themselves.

The basic needs a human being lives for is the needs for *physiological satisfaction* in areas of food, clothing, shelter. If a person has this insufficiency, they will then feel the motivation to achieve needs for *safety and security*. If a teenager lives in a risky and violent environment, they will feel the need to protect themselves first in order to feel safe. This explains why teenagers from violent upbringing develop some violence related habits and characters.

The next level of needs is the need to be *loved and have a sense of belonging.*

This is the desire that pushes for the formation of friendships and relationships that a person/ a teenager will feel accepted and loved. If a teenager feels unloved and unaccepted at home, they will look for places where they will feel more loved, and it might not come as a shock when they end up having the wrong friends and engaging in drugs. The friends they find will in most cases have similar needs as them, and this will bond them.

The next level of needs has to do with a person's *self-esteem*. A person who has met the above needs will feel the need to have an accomplishment and recognition/prestige. This is mostly the reason why teenagers who lack recognition from their parents or the people they live with struggle with self-esteem. They feel like they have inadequacy to accomplish anything purposeful in life for which they can find recognition. As a result, they will engage in extreme activities that call for attention and recognition, and they will find pride in such actions.

The final and highest level of needs has to do with a person's *self-actualization*. This need refers to the feeling to achieve the best of your innate ability or their full potential. The person who has this desire will have met all the other needs we saw above.

Based on the theory of Abraham Maslow, a teenager with unmet psychological desires will find trouble in feeling any motivation in relation to academic achievements. These children will mostly have psychological disorders. A person can stagnate at a certain level of needs until such needs are met.

Tips to helping your child attain a healthy self-esteem

There are certain techniques you can put in place to help your child develop a healthy view of themselves. Teenagers are very sensitive when it comes to their perception, and they will place their personal value on what their parents and the people they live with say about them.

You can participate in certain family activities collectively and ban the use of mobile phones while at it.

Encourage your child to work on this talent and help them discover what they are good at. Parents should also support their teenagers in establishing their talents and making them realize that their success in life is not solely determined by academic excellence. Children are talented in different ways, but the schooling system lowers the self-esteem of children with low grades in class. This tactic will work in such a case to give the child something they excel at.

It is also helpful to teach your teenager child that it's okay to fail at times and whenever they fail, they still have another opportunity to try again. Failure in different areas, such as competitions can be demotivating to a child. The parents should come in and give their unconditional support to the teenager and encourage them to be resilient.

Let your daughter understand that they are beautiful without any makeup. The appearance of a teenager is very important as they keep comparing themselves to others. The use of makeup can become obsessive to a teenager.

The value a parent places on themselves affects their teenagers. Do not put your insecurities before your children. Teenagers and smaller children tend to copy the habits of their parents.

Unleashing your child's talents to change the world

There are certain tactics a parent can use to realize and nurture the talents of their children.

Help your child discover what they are good at. Through your child's development, you will notice certain activities that excited the child and which if given the required support they can excel in. A parent should help a child in the thinking process to figure out which activities they find interest in and focus more attention on them.

Let the ideas of interest come from the child but not father parents. As parents, most of the time, you will have dreams and desires for your children, but those are your desires, not theirs. Owing to this, you should let your child follow their own interests and support whatever it is they choose to do. Be it sports, music, among other talents.

Parents should hone the talents of their children. The perfection of talent will require continuous practice through a process error. The parents of a teen in the process of discussion should teach the children how to stay on track and motivate them to try again every time they encounter failure. Parents should provide the necessary support in terms of facilities and equipment to help their children perfect their talents to the maximum. If training is required, the parents should be ready to provide that too. Every effort a child makes should be applauded to encourage them to keep going.

Do not discourage your child from copying professionals in the field they find interesting. That will be a good start for the child as they discover their own way.

How to motivate teens and support them in their decisions

A teenager, as we saw earlier, has developed the ability to make a decision. Being supportive in the decisions our children make will help them trust the parents' love. However, proper guidance should be given by reasoning together to figure out if the decision is the best. Help your child through the thinking process by asking them open-ended questions which will help them reason through all the options available.

It is important to note that our children are different from us and their interest and ours might differ. For this reason, don't push or pressure a child into doing some activity just because you think they might be good at it. By providing a wide range of opportunities, a child will definitely find the one which they find interest in.

We can help our children more by listening to their ideas and helping them work out the decision they make. A teenager who decides to quit his or her part-time job will obviously have a reason behind it. As a parent, we should provide a listening ear without rushing to pass judgment or refute their decision.

It is also important to train our children to work towards achieving certain goals. A parent can do this by helping the child work out short term and long term goals. This will help them have targets and work hard to beat the targets. Targets also offer a way of challenging the child to achieve more competitively, encourage your child to do better than before, but if they fail, we should help them stay positive. It is easy for a child to get discouraged whenever they find difficulties in doing something. However, it is helpful if we choose to help the child give another try. The setting of goals also trains a child to be self-motivated in achieving excellence in other areas of life.

Motivation comes with a reward. Whenever your child accomplishes a certain goal, a parent should reward the child or let the child know that you are proud of the achievements.

A parent should teach the child to keep trying and doing their best and not fear failure. Most children will be disappointed wherever they fail, which is quite natural. However, our attitude as parents towards our child's failure will determine if they will be willing to try again or just give it up altogether. Allow your child to make mistakes because mistakes are part of the learning process. Through mistakes, a child will be able to know what doesn't work.

Mistakes as a learning process for your child

We should teach our children to acknowledge the mistakes they do and take full ownership. Owning up to a mistake takes courage and promote the levels of maturity of a person. We can explain and let our children understand that owning up to a mistake is not weakness; instead, it attracts respect. As parents owning up to our own mistakes will also make it easier for our children to admit they are wrong.

The next thing a person should do once they realizes they made a mistake is to try to make things right. Teaching our children to amend mistakes is a way of promoting healthy behaviors associated with responsible adults. This will also help your child to be resilient when they encounter challenging situations in life. While at fixing the mistake another mistake might occur but a parent should reassure their children that it's still okay as long as they don't give up they will finally get it right.

Help your child analyze the cause of the mistake in terms of answering why, what, and when of the mistake. Through figuring out the cause, a similar mistake can be avoided in the future.

Help your child put the lessons learned into practice. Trying over and over again will lead to innovation and perfection.

Chapter 3: How to Communicate with Your Son

The kind of communication that a child develops with a parent determines how they relate. As a child grows to a teenager, sometimes, they find difficulties in opening up to their parents. The once-close relationship with parents shifts to their friends and peers. Friends become an essential part of the child's lives. The society has set expectations on how men should act, and they are accorded with responsibilities, and they are not expected to show high levels of attachment to their parents. Men from an early age, are socialized to independent lives free from showing emotions in the worst of situations. As boys grow into men their relationship with parents diverges more as compared to girls.

Role of Parents in their Son's Life

Mother's role

Mothers are created with a softness related to naturist of children. Mothers role in a son's life is much softer as compared to a father's.

Sons acquire emotional intelligence form their mothers. It has been proven that children raised by their mothers since birth are less problematic in terms of behaviors. A mother gives the son a sense of safety and makes him more confident in himself. On the other hand, sons whose mothers were absent in their early years of growth tend to show aggression and hostility as they grow up.

The love of a mother raises self-esteem in a son by assuring him that he is cared for.

Being raised by a mother trains a child how to treat women with respect. It also happens that these men can form successful relationships because they can express themselves better and without fear of being emotional.

A mother helps a son develop excellent communication skills that help the child throughout his life.

Children raised by their mothers are more responsible and hardly engage in extreme behavior.

Father's Role

Father's raise their sons differently from the mother. Unknown to many parents, sons are always seeking approval from their fathers. The father, being the head of the family, is the son's biggest role model. The responsibility of fatherhood is the greatest form of exercising masculinity. The skills a son acquires from the father are quite distinct from those from the mother, and they include: independence as fathers are less attached to the child at the same time loving him immensely. Fathers teach their sons how to deal with difficulties in life, being bold and brave by taking up life challenges, and also what entails the opposite gender relationship. Judging from the way a man treats women; including his wife, mother, sisters, the son will form relationship status based on such. For instance, if a father beats the mother or is abusive towards the mother, the son will treat his wife is a more similar way.

The father is the biggest role model for the son on different aspects of life ranging from how he should treat his family and how to be a man. Most men are always in search of ways to get to their fathers' good side and earn his love. Being a role model means that most boys grow up to be like their fathers.

Sons view their fathers as a source of security. Most children see their fathers as the most powerful person they know, and boys look at their father's strength with admiration. Fathers are also the disciplinarians in their sons' lives. Society sees fathers as providers. This is the traditional role of a father. Men are made with more strength to fend for their families.

How do you make your son listen to you without screaming?

Communication with adolescents, especially boys is rather hard. Trying to communicate with an unresponsive child can be so frustrating causing the parents to scream opacity them which hardly works. Here are some strategies that might be helpful to help you engage in a healthy conversation with your son.

- You should notify the child in advance that you intend to talk to him and tell him what you intend to talk about. This will leave him psychologically prepared for the conversation and leave him enough time to go over what you will be discussing. The child will also come up with issues they want both of you to go over while at it.

- Before you set out on the conversation, make sure that the child has had something to eat. Hunger can lead to diverted attention and irritable behavior.
- Keep your wording short and to the point. Too long conversations are rather boring to teenage boys. Their attention can be easily diverted to the surrounding and other thoughts that might recur in mind. Also, aim at a dialogue form of communication. Keeping a calm tone and asking questions will work in getting a teenage boy to talk.
- Stay calm as you have your conversation.
- Boys get easily distracted, walking as you talk can prove helpful.
- Avoid certain nonverbal communication cues such as eye contact which a child might interpret as an attack and result in forming some defensive mechanisms that block out the conversation leading to a dead end.
- Use some real-life examples that will make the conversation memorable.
- Let your son understand that you support him before you get started on the conversation to bring down any walls he might have created in anticipation for an attack.
- It is important to give your child time to go over the conversation if you don't get the results you anticipated. After giving him sometime, you can recall the conversation you had with him and seek the answers you needed. The child might surprise you with rather unexpected suggestions.

What approach to adopt: a rigid, protective, or friendly parent

Authoritarian Parenting

It is also referred to as a *rigid form of parenting* where the parents are extremely strict with the expectations their eyes set out for their children.

Children born of these parents are socialized not to question the authority of their parents. Little or no communication exists between parents and children. Strict rules are set out, which must be followed to the letter and failure to meet the rules punishment is always awaiting. Spanking of children is very common in this form of parenting. Most of the parents who use this technique were raised by similar parents. The consequences of this parenting technique are:

- The child develops a very negative attitude towards people in authority.
- It brings about children with low self-esteem.
- Children raised by such parents tend to act out.
- It brings about children with anger management problems.
- Children have deep resentment and withheld frustrations.
- The children find difficulties in building up healthy social lives.
- It gives the children an urgency to conform.
- Children from such homes find difficulties in independent decision making.

Why psychologists find this parenting style unproductive

A child should be raised in a way that they can control their own actions and not driven by fear. This will build on their levels of independence in decision making and healthy self-esteem.

In this parenting style, children don't feel loved and valued by their parents.

The administration of strong punishment on children makes them feel unloved and they retaliate with rebellion.

The punishment awarded to children is meant to correct them not to create fear in them.

The guidelines set out by parents should be aimed at leading the child in the right direction but not a way of exercising authority over them.

Permissive Parenting / Protective Parenting

This is a form of parenting characterized by very relaxed parenting skills. A permissive or protective parent will easily give in to the child's demands as a way to avoid conflict with the child. A parent using this parenting technique will use material items to control the behavior of their children. Children raised in such backgrounds are often manipulative to the parents whenever they need certain demands to be addressed. The consequences of this parenting technique are:

- Underage alcoholics and substance abuse
- Tendencies of acting out and aggression.
- Children mostly find them in conflict with authority because they are not used to having rules.
- Children develop self-centeredness and sense of entitlement.
- It brings about children without self-discipline.

Positive/friendly Parenting

This parenting technique is established on a loving and caring background. Parents who practice this technique are always planning ahead on the children future and providing the necessary support emotionally, physically and psychologically while allowing their children to make quality decisions. This is the most recommended parenting technique because it gives the child a strong background in the future.

The perspective of this parenting technique involves:

Desirable character development. This is done through modeling. Parents establish and layout guidelines and principles that they would like to see their children emulate within themselves. Children learn to respect their parents as they see them leading by example.

The parent should practice positive parenting discipline. This involves the application of appropriate consequences for inappropriate actions from your children. Rather than using coercion, the discipline methods applied are a learning process for the child. A parent uses appropriate discipline procedures that involve communication to help your child understand the consequences of their actions and the need for change.

Discipline is done by:

- A strong United family front aimed at finding solutions. Rather than coercion.
- A parent should not be majoring on what the child did wrong but what he does right.
- Acknowledging your child's achievements and letting the child

know that you are proud of them.

- The application of appropriate communication methods to understand how your child feels and how you can meet their needs by listening to them and empathizing.
- The parent should be loving, caring and warm enough for the child to be able to open up and communicate without fear of being judged and accused.
- Both the parents and children have healthy levels of trust, respect each other and are supportive of each other in all aspects of life; starting from the simple home chores.
- The parents help the child in making positive decisions which are not damaging to their future.
- Cultivating a culture of autonomous in your child and trusting them enough to involve them in making a decision that has on matters that have a direct impact on their lives.

This parenting technique builds on a child's self-esteem and instills values that are attributed to a successful life. Parents using this technique benefit from it as it structures their lives in a positive way by reinforcing desirable values and attributes in themselves. Through this strategy, a child develops into a responsible adult who is capable of making sound decisions and leading a quality life. Additionally, the home environment is warm and welcoming, which promotes unity among the family members. It is important to note that this parenting technique starts as early as the family begins forming for it to be effective.

Taking the Son's Side

A parent's instinct will most often compel you to side with the son. As much as you need your child to understand that you love them and that you will always be supportive, certain situations require a parent to have their foot down. A son should know that inappropriate behaviors attract certain levels of responsibility as much as they know the parent loves them.

It helps a child's esteem when you are supportive of his decisions and gives the appropriate support to enable them to succeed. The parenting technique you use on your son will determine the kind of relationship you have with your child. You can love your child without letting him walk all over you by establishing a strong value structure in the family from the moment the child is born.

In parenting, unity between the parents is very important. According to research, the son can read the differences between parents and use that to their advantage. Parents who unite in giving appropriate punishment to children are less likely to experience rebellion. However, if one partner chooses to side with the son while the other is trying to point out inappropriate behaviors the success of parenting that child is doomed. Parents should lay out guidelines for raising children right from the start and follow them strictly to establish a formal family structure.

Whenever parents make their personal differences obvious to a child, the child takes advantage of them and finds opportunities to escape punishment and pick behaviors they desire. In most cases, a son can turn the tables on a parent and get away with it without facing any consequences. Even when the parents have different opinions, their son should not get an insight into the problems facing the couple. In this case, the couple should put the children first and agree on a united parenting style that does not affect the moral development of the son.

Parents should also prevent criticizing each other's parenting technique in front of their sons. The children will pick up such information and build a different image of their parents that lower the levels of respect. In these cases, a couple is showing their disrespect of each other in front of their children. The levels of the couple are being lowered to that of the child and this will definitely lead to problems for the child in following instructions from the parents.

Don't act on the schemes set by the company

What this refers to is not to let your son be the one to guide you. A child from an early age learn their parents and establish a way to control their parents in pursuit of their freedom and desires. The parenting technique is very important in developing levels of respect. Guidelines that will help a parent to establish healthy levels of respect from their children;

- Whenever your son misbehaves, don't overreact rather try to stay calm.
- Give appropriate levels of respect to your children.

- Acknowledge your own mistakes and apologize.
- Your moral and personal values should be modeling to your son.

Let your children understand the structure of expected behavior and how that contributes to molding their future. When the child understands the sense behind your demands on the behavior, they will simply flow with it without need for coercion which brings about retaliation.

The discipline procedures used by parents affect the attitude of the child. A parent should train the child to follow what is right without punishing him. Positive discipline methods help the child learn why what they did was wrong and how to behave in the right way.

Chapter 4: Teenagers and Divorce

The event of divorce leads to a lot of mixed feelings for the children. The rate of divorce has gone very high in recent years, and it follows that 4 to 6 out of every ten married couple go through a divorce. The changes in life after divorce pose a challenge to the children, and it follows that parents will even find it hard to formulate a workable co-parenting plan.

The more parents cooperate in the parenting even after divorce, the easier it gets for the children to adjust. Researchers have found out that children of divorce are norepinephrine likely to rebel and misbehave.

The Relationship between Separated Parents and Children

The relationship between children of divorce shifts in different ways. The presence of one parent in their lives reduced, and this affects how the children relate to both parents.

For teenagers, divorce leads to feelings of resentment towards the parents, and they may end up blaming one of the parents for the divorce. However, there are other cases where divorce leads to relief to the children in cases where the parents were constantly in disagreement, and the home was defined by chaos.

The custodian of the children in the event of a divorce will often face difficulties in controlling the children. The parent will, in most cases, raise the children with permissive parenting where behavior monitoring is not put into much consideration. The parent is mostly overwhelmed by the stress, and at the same time, the children don't experience the same levels of love they are used to with both parents. The discipline might not be effective because of such factors.

Here are some measures that parents can put in place while going through a divorce to ensure the children have a smooth transition:

- After divorce, parents should maintain a good relationship with each other for the sake of the children. It is easier said than done, but it is not impossible.
- The emotions that come with a divorce are quite high, and despite

the feelings of anger and resentment, parents should avoid talking negative sentiments about each other in the presence of the children.

- Issues of child support should be discussed away from the children.
- One parent should not use the children to hurt the other. Telling children details about the other parent is also another mistake that parents make.
- It is important to allow the children to continue having a healthy satisfactory relationship with the other parent.
- Each parent should live up to their promises regarding the children wellbeing and always show unconditional support
- Work on a selfless parenting plan that does not favor any given side.
- Maintain a consistent plan in raising your children in order to set up a strict and predictable environment for the children's security.
- Both parents should be involved in all the aspects of the child's growth, such as schooling and other activities the child is involved in.
- Ensure that the children understand that you love them and you will always be there for them. While at it, let them know that the divorce has got nothing to do with them so that they don't blame themselves.
- Without mentioning unnecessary details, give the children the information they require.
- The news about the divorce should be delivered to the child by both parents.
- It is also advisable for divorced parents to seek professional help for themselves in order to be in good health emotionally and sound enough psychologically to raise the children.
- Parents should also monitor their teenage children closely in the event of divorce. The stress and emotions that come with divorce might divert the attention of a parent from the children leading to them engaging in extremely dangerous activities.
- Parents should equip their children with the skills they need, such as critical decision making, which will help them cope well with the changes taking place in relation to the divorce.

- The discipline of the children should be structured and consistent even after divorce.
- If you notice that your child has changed or the divorce has taken a toll on him, it is advisable to seek professional help for the child as soon as possible to alleviate the risk of developing a mental health problem.

How Divorce Affects Children

In cases of divorce, the parenting technique matters in determining how the divorce affects the children. It is also important to reduce the levels of conflict; especially the ones affecting the children because they will feel it. The children should also be able to feel the presence of both parents in their lives.

Divorce results in diverse effects that parents contemplating divorce should have in mind and work through it. In the event of a divorce, the children always bear the burden in the following ways:

- Children of divorce are more likely to engage in extreme behavior and habits such as drugs and substance abuse and early engagement in sexual activities.
- The children who were raised by their separated parents tend to have difficulty in building romantic relationships and a huge percentage of the end up divorced.
- Research has associated the children from divorced parents as having difficulties in school, which affect their performances as compared to those of stable backgrounds.
- Mental health problems are higher in children whose parents are divorced as compared to those living with both parents.

How to Communicate Separation

Divorce is a very key event in the lives of children. The perception the child holds on divorce all depends on how you approach the topic when breaking the news to the children. There are certain tactics parents can use to break the news to the children more effectively:

Only inform your children of impending divorce when you are already finalized your decision to get divorced. Telling children of possibilities will only work at stressing them with an uncertain future.

The parents should break the news to the children together. This will reduce the chances of the children getting conflicting information as well as letting them understated the divorce was arrived at from mutual agreement. It is important to have a plan on how you will break the news and what to say to the children to communicate effectively with minimum emotional effects. Be truthful in giving information to kids keeping in mind their ages to tell them only what they need to know. The children will definitely have questions which you should be ready to answer with utmost honesty.

Avoid blaming each other for the failed marriage, and instead, both parents should take responsibility for the failure. It also follows that the children don't need to know your marriage problems and financial difficulties. When you criticize your ex in front of the children, remember that's the mother or father to the child, and they have a deep attachment, for this reason, it leaves the child confused on what actions to take.

As you break the news to your children, keep it simple and avoid the details. Keep the divorce papers away from the children. Any other conversations relating to the divorce should be had away from the children.

The information about divorce is not light on a child because it will mean an irreversible change in their lives. By closely keeping watch of your children, you will be able to notice how the information affects them. You can reassure them of your unconditional love and duck support. The children also need to know that it's not their fault that the parents are getting separated.

Finally, the parents need to seek counseling in order to heal for the feelings and emotions that come with the divorce from a dysfunctional marriage. A healthy mental, emotional state, and physical being will enable you to give your children the support they need to get through that stressful phase in their lives.

Creating a Relationship of Trust and Respect After Separation

Divorce affects every member of the family, and relationships between children and parents change. However, these relationships can be restructured.

- Avoid discussing matters that led to the divorce with your children. It simply isn't their business to worry about.
- Avoid uttering negative comments about your ex in the presence of your children.
- It is not acceptable to send the children with messages to the other parent or interrogate them concerning the other parent.
- Monitor the progress of your children closely. Children of divorce are at a higher risk of engaging in unruly behavior.
- Participate fully in the life of your children, giving them the necessary support make the child a major part of your life.
- Encourage your child to lead the normal life he led before the divorce happened. Encourage their social life and friends and other hobbies and activities they used to engage in before the divorce.
- Dedicate your time for your children. This will help them understand that you love them, and despite the separation as parents, you haven't divorced the children.
- Offer your children a listening ear. Be attentive to the children concerns and address them appropriately. When children realize they will be listened to, they communicate more.
- Practice consistency and predictability in your dealings with your children. This will help establish a concrete structure for the children with a more stable environment.
- Don't rush to introduce a new romantic partner to your children unless you are sure the relationship is stable; another failed relationship will lead to more distress to the children. Even after getting a new partner, always remember to put your children first.

Creating a Healthy Relationship with Your Ex for the Benefit of the Children:

Children like stability and predictability in their lives. Constant conflicts, on the other hand, have a huge negative effect on the lives of children. Parents who have been divorced should focus on developing a healthy relationship, which will be helpful in co-parenting. Let us look at ways you can maintain a healthy relationship with your ex even after divorce.

Each parent should acknowledge their own contribution to the separation. It is always the responsibility of both partners to keep a marriage intact, and when it false apart, both parents will have played a part in it. Admitting to the faults one committed helps in healing and forgiveness even if the divorce is irreversible; they will live in harmony with less bitterness towards each other.

It is important to make amendments with your partner for the lies you might have schemed during the divorce proceedings to attain an advantage over your partner. Returning something you took illegally can work in diffusing the anger and building a more friendly relationship.

If you can't say anything positive about your partner, don't say it. Most exes make a mistake of slandering each other to the adolescent worse state of affairs than it was before the divorce. If you already said it, try being positive and speak of the good qualities of the other person to create a balance in opinions.

In case you had put the children in the midst of the divorce or if you were using the children to get back at your ex, just stop. Your ex will appreciate having a healthy relationship with the children, and though they may not acknowledge it verbally they will have a more relaxed attitude towards you.

If you are trying to go back to dating, you should not date someone just to punish your ex emotionally. Maintain boundaries with people close to your ex; like friends and relatives are involved. Date for your own happiness but not as a way of revenge for the promiscuity of your ex while you were still together.

You can choose to have a respectful distance between the two of you after divorce or even choose to stay in the social circle of friends. Either way, it is important to respect each other and maintain a healthy relationship that will leave the children with a more emotionally stable environment for their own development.

Maintaining Our Responsibilities

When parents divorce, the responsibility of raising the children born in the union lies with both parents unless the court decides to give the responsibility to one partner. A child of at least 12 years can make a request in court to be under the responsibility of one parent. However, each child is ruled on individually.

Co-parenting is an arrangement whereby both parents come up with an agreement on how they will equally share the responsibility of raising the children. The law does not provide for any form of regulation concerning co-parenting. However, the parents decide between themselves on how they would share the costs and who stays with the children and when.

If one partner doesn't owner their end of the bargain, then you can file for a case in court and the courts can decide on the appropriate measures.

Chapter 5: Teens and Sex

The sex topic is uncomfortable to discuss with your child. It is even more uncomfortable for the child. However, it is important to have this healthy conversation with your adolescents as early as teenage kicks in. However, the sex talk is a continuous conversation that you go over and over again as your child gets older.

Why is it important for parents to engage their teenagers on the sex talk?

The world today, in the form of the different media, is full of sex information. If you don't talk to your child appropriately about sex, he or she will acquire the information elsewhere, and it might be misleading. With the high levels of hormones and their bodies' development, teens might feel the urge to experiment on what they see on media. By talking to your child about sex, you ensure that the child gets the right information.

Through this conversation, the child will be able to value their bodies more and have a good understanding how the body parts function.

When you have a sex talk with your child, you are opening up room for open communication. From this conversation, your children will feel free to talk to you about the problems they go through and the situations that pose challenges.

This is also an opportunity to set up the values you desire for your children to live up to. Whatever information you give your child will determine their attitude towards sex.

Communication is also a way of bonding with your child. As you talk, you will find your child asking questions that they would have otherwise kept to themselves. As we have said, the sex talk is a continuous conversation; when a child finds a romantic partner, they will be freer to let you meet him or her.

This talk also opens up a teenager's mind on the expectations of a future spouse and the dating process. It will enable the child to rule out partners who would be damaging to their future based on the values you build in your child.

With the appropriate information, a child is less likely to engage in early sex out of curiosity, and if your child does engage in sexual activity, he or she will know how to do it safely to avoid certain related risks such as early pregnancies and infection with sexually transmitted diseases.

How to Communicate with Your Child About Sex

The sex talk starts at an early age whereby the parents create awareness of the child's sexuality. At different ages, parents can give their children information regarding what's appropriate behavior and what's not. A child of 2 to 5 years should be informed that he or she should not allow people to touch them inappropriately and if someone touches them inappropriately, they should go to the parents with such information. A child at this age is also curious about certain matters like the formation of babies. As a parent, you will find yourself being asked such questions and it is important not to lie to your child. Lying to your child labels you as a liar, and that's not a way of establishing trust with your children. At this age, children are in a talking stage, and you have the responsibility as a parent to give them the names of the different body parts but at the same time avoid attaching those arts to a specific gender. Just tell them the names of the body parts they have and they should not be showing the body parts in public. Wherever your child starts touching his private parts in public you should tell him gently that he can only do that in private and if he feels any kind of discomfort, he or she should tell you about it.

Since from the age 6 to 8 years, children can read and access the internet, parents should inform the child of the certain sites they should not be accessing and what kind of materials they should avoid looking at. A child of this age should know not to share their photographs on the Internet; they should also know it's inappropriate to talk to strangers or be touched by strangers. At this age, a child will be starting to get curious about their bodies, and it is important to talk to them about the changes they should expect to occur to their bodies and explain it's a normal process of growth that does not have to be scary but embraced. A child of this age should also be aware of sexual abuse. However, the sexual abuse topic should be discussed gradually. At first, you can inform them what sexual abuse entails and that they should not have people touching their bodies inappropriately, then you can explain it in depth as you progress depending on how much your child can understand.

A child of 9 to 12 years is already experiencing certain changes in his or her body. Do not wait until it is too late to talk to your child about her menses. While at the talk, do not leave out any details. Let your child know that their bodies are now developed enough to been parents. The talk about safe sex should also come in for both boys and girls. Teenagers with information about the safety of sex and its importance will not risk having unprotected sex. Romantic relationships also start forming at this stage, do not scare your child from being in a relationship but let the child know that even when you have a boyfriend or girlfriend, there is an appropriate time for sex and they should wait until they are mature enough. Explain to the child that sex is an act of love and commitment which is most appropriate in marriage. The child should also know the repercussions of engaging in early sex in detail but do not scare the child.

Having Sex Talk with Teenagers

When discussing the sex topic with teenagers, it's important to be so brief and straight to the point. It is important to hold in mind that your teenage child might already be sexually active. Researchers have found out that children who get sex information from an early age are less likely to go into early sexual practices.

What to talk about with your teenage child with regard to sex?

Choice of friends. A parent needs to address the behaviors of a teenage based on the choice of friends your child has. When having this conversation, you should address the role friends play in molding a person's future. You could make the child understand how to get good role models for the person they aspire to be. You can use tangible evidence from your own life.

- *Waiting for the appropriate time to engage in sex.* Though there is no set time for when a person should start engaging in sex, it is advisable to encourage your child to engage in sex when married. You should instill values that will create an attitude of abstinence until they are mature enough and are ready to start up families.
- *The use of contraception.* At this age, children are aware of what entails sex, and some of them are even considering having romantic partners. Every parent hopes that their child abstains

from sex. However, this might not be possible with your child. The media and peers play an important role in pressuring your child to experiment and explore their sexuality. The media itself gives teenagers imagination and fantasies that are far from reality. The introduction of the use of different types of contraception making more emphasis on condoms. The child needs to know all the risks involved with contraception so make them aware that there is no 100% effective contraception. A condom can burst; this is something a teenager should be made aware of. All in all, encourage the child to wait for the most appropriate time to have sex.

- *Sexually transmitted diseases*. A teenager should be aware of the different types of sexually transmitted diseases and how they are transmitted along with how they can be prevented. When you have the sex talk with your teenage child, don't leave out the information about the risks involved in sex. The child should be informed about the symptoms of diseases and when to see a doctor. Most teenagers, when infected with sexually transmitted diseases, will find difficulties in seeking help. These frequent conversations with your child might help them in opening up and sharing some problems they might be experiencing in their lives.

- *Early pregnancies*. Among the risks of unsafe sex, pregnancy is the most feared in teenage. What teenagers should be aware of is that this is not the worst outcome of unique protected sex. However, you should make your child aware of the cost related to early pregnancies, how it changes the lives of the girls in particular, and the responsibility associated with raising a child.

Empowering your child with decision-making skills will enable them to choose the right pathways in life. Equipped with all the information your child needs to know regarding sex, they can make an informed decision. Even if they choose to engage in sex, they will know how to be safe around it.

If your child is already sexually active

If you discover that your child is engaging in early sex, it is important to verify the source of information. Unless the child comes to you with the information, you will need to be certain that you have accurate information. Trust between parents and their children is very important. Though we are advised to keep close watch of our children, we should set boundaries which do not allow us to invade their privacy. If you invade a child's privacy such as going through their telephone messages, even if you get such information you can't go straight to them with it because there will be no trust. The child needs to know you can trust them enough to make the right choices. If you pry into their personal space, they will keep some distance from you and look for ways to conceal information from the parent. The regular sex talk should be a way of getting your child to open up if they are facing a challenge.

If you find out your child is already engaging in sex, don't panic. Look for the most appropriate time to indulge in the topic. While at it, however much disappointed you are about the occurrence, don't show it to the child. Overreacting and throwing accusations will only make the issue worse. Teenagers require a calm atmosphere to open up and give information.

It is important to listen more than just keep talking. Listen to what your child has to say about the issue and the person with whom they had the encounter. Encourage your child to tell you how they feel about the experience and the person as well as the future plans. If they intend to continue with the relationship or otherwise. The less you talk the more information you can get without asking any leading questions. It is important to acknowledge that you can't control the sexual behaviors of your child it is a decision they make on their own. From the communication you have with your child, you can tell what they are looking for? If they engaged in unprotected sex within a span of hours you could advise them on the health measures to take.

The fact that your child started engaging in sex does not mean they have to keep doing it. You need to make them aware of that. They can choose to abstain from there onwards. Depending on the encounter, your child needs your emotional support. First-time sexual encounters could lead to psychological distress; especially if your child was pressured to sex. Counseling might be an alternative choice if your child appears traumatized. Such encounters can taint the opinion and attitude your child holds on sex leading to adverse effects stretching to their future relationships with the opposite sex.

Sons should also be aware of the importance off the use of contraception. Bring your son to understand the responsibilities that are demanded of the father as per the law. However, they should know that only a mother can decide on abortion and if they got a girl pregnant and she decides to keep the child, the father has no way around it but assume the responsibility of fatherhood. Boys should understand they are equally responsible for the child's upkeep as the mother.

How to Handle the Different Impacts of Unprotected Sex Concerning Our Children

When the worst comes to happen, your child might contract some illnesses or pregnancies. Here is an outline of the information you could find useful in dealing with the situation:

The first step a parent should take in the most disappointing of all situations is to stay as calm about the situation as possible. Overreacting will lead to heightened emotions that's will not help in resolving the situation. Bringing your child to understand what they should anticipate is a safe step to take in resolving the issue. The parents should understand that the child is going through worse emotional distress than them. Calmly bring your child to talk about what they are going through and the need to see a clinician.

Give your child the support they need in taking care of the situation. If your child is ill, you should take the child to the hospital and provide all the requirements to get them back a normal life. Let the child know that you are not pleased with the situation, but you love him or her regardless. No child wants to frustrate their parents' expectations.

Lay down all the options your child has in case it is a pregnancy. The decision your child takes will also affect you as a parent, but even with this in mind, don't decide for them. Give them all the options available, as well as the time they need to decide what they think is the best option for them. Avoid pressuring them into making a decision.

Let your child understand the value of education in the future of themselves and their children. As a parent, give your child the support they require to stay in school. Mothers who have children in teenage years are more likely to lead a life of poverty because most of them drop out of school. Researchers have also confirmed that the likelihood of a teen having more than one child is very high.

Finally, your child needs professional help to come to terms with the situation. If your daughter is pregnant, abortion or childbearing can be traumatizing at an early age. It is important to make sure that your daughter sees a therapist to help her go through the experience and come out with more lessons than regrets.

If your child decides to have the child, it is important to ensure them having a normal life as much as possible in order for them to achieve their goals. You can explore support groups that engage teen mums to be part of.

The father of the child should take up some responsibilities to help the girl and her family. He should also be present physically to give the girl emotional support as well as getting to interact with the child when it is born.

Despite your support, when the child is born, let the mother nurture the child. Remember your role is that of a grandparent but offer her all the support she requires in raising the child. If you neglect your child, she will go into the vicious cycle of poverty with your grandchild.

If your daughter has a child as a teenager, your other girl children might fall into the same trap. To avoid this, take early precautions and figure out where you went wrong in parenting to make things right with the other siblings.

Chapter 6: Teens and Social Problems

The problems our teenagers are facing today can be attributed to the changes in technology, more so the social media. The daily life of an average teenager revolves around social media. There are several social problems currently facing teenagers in the society which include:

Depression

Children are more prone to depression than ever before. We have looked at depression in details in the first chapter of this book. The use of social media is among the major causes of depression among teenagers. Parents need to watch the behavior of their teenagers closely and if they notice changes in behavior that may suggest depression, seek professional help for the child. Depression is also a leading cause of suicide among teens.

Bullying

This has become an ongoing issue among teenagers. The cause is mainly attributed to the low levels of empathy among teens. Parents should constantly talk to their children about bullying. Inform your child how to act when encountering a bully or an incident of someone being bullied. It is also important to know as a parent how to act if your child is a bully.

There are several types of bullying: sexual bullying, verbal bullying, cyberbullying, and aggression (physical and relational).

How to recognize bullying:

Bullies have a higher level of power, some physically or/and psychologically. A bully will capitalize on their power to put down devour their victims. They might be bigger or have a higher social status as compared to their victims, which gives them a feeling of superiority. The bullies target those weaker than them.

Bullying follows a recurrent pattern where the oppressor attacks the victim in a certain way repeatedly for a period of time.

Bullying happens on purpose, with the intent to harm the victim. This can be by words, through the social media posts, physically or psychologically. They also tend to create fear in the victim.

How to Prevent Your Child from being Bullied

A parent should teach their children how to stand up for themselves against bullies. This comes with self-confidence, which you can also help a child develop. A parent who raises their child with a comfortable level of self-esteem hardly has to deal with such problems. It is important to let your child understand that most bullies have low self-esteem and they use their power to boost their ego. Most of the children being bullied are good at something which the bully might not be able to stand. If you make your child aware of their unique abilities, they can even gather the confidence to walk away from the bullies unharmed. Another important point to keep in mind is that the bullies are often cowards. It takes a little standing up to them to cower them away.

A child should be able to respect himself or herself and others. Respect for others and oneself will keep off bullies. This is because they can't access any weak points of penetrating to your child.

A child should always report any incidents of bullying to the parents and other authorities. Bullies instill fear in their victims, which might prevent a child from reporting the cases to authority. However, as a parent, you should let your child understand that when they fail to report, the bullying will continue.

Self-confidence can help a child avoid incidents of bullying. You should teach your child to love and appreciate the unique person he or she is. Bullies target people for being different. It does not come as a surprise that most bright students are bullied for being too focused on their academics. If your child can proudly embrace their uniqueness, bullies will not find any way of getting through to them.

Ensure that no bullying goes on in your home. In some families, you might find that smaller children are being taken advantage of by the big ones to a great extent, which can be looked at as bullying. A parent should pay keen attention to what happens at home by closely examining the complaints from the smaller children. If a child is being bullied at home, they develop fear and low self-esteem which will attract bullies elsewhere. At the same time, a parent might be unknowingly raising a bully in their own house.

Why do people bully others?

The items bullies point at in their victims are not always a weakness. A bully has insecurities that are too weighty for him or her, and prefers to cover them up by pulling others lower than them.

A child will be bullied for various reasons; however, it is important to let the child know that it is not their fault that they are being bullied. Among these reasons are:

As a result of trauma or stress

Unfortunately, those people who bully others according to research findings have been through some traumatizing experience which they don't know how to deal with. To cover up for their feelings, these people go bullying others. Bullying others, however, doesn't make the trauma go away. If your child is showing g signs of a bully, it is important to have him or her see by a specialist. You could also look at your child's past five years' experience and see what might be causing the trauma or stress and have it dealt with as early as possible.

Societal acquired aggressive behavior in men.

The society has built certain expectations of men whereby they are supposed to be strong and not show emotions. When a child is brought up with such values, the only way they can show emotions is through being aggressive.

Bullies have low self-esteem

People who bully others are, in a way, trying to deflect the attention they feel directed to their own weaknesses to other people. This means that by bullying others, they feel that their shortcomings are not visible and these habits tend to emasculate them by making them feel good about themselves. Their feelings of inferiority are curbed by their ability to bring others down.

Others will bully others as payback

It has been discovered that most people who bully others have been bullied themselves at some point in their lives. Most of these people believe that by bullying others, they themselves will not be bullied which is not the case.

Problems resulting from home

Most children bullies come for large families where attention is limited. Others have been raised in homes where they don't live with close relatives, and they suffer from feelings of rejection.

Children from violent backgrounds tend to turn the same attitude on others; this is because it's the only way they know how to live.

Lack of understanding

This is more common with people from low education backgrounds who don't find any wrongdoing in hurling negative statements at others.

Peer pressure

Some children bully others as a way of trying to fit in certain groups of bullies. Through bullying, they gain acceptance by the perceived leaders of the group. Others will just bully others to satisfy the group's criteria of BP being accepted though they are not comfortable doing it.

Cyberbullying

This is another type of bullying that applies the use of technology to put down someone through photographs and demeaning comments. Cyberbullying can be carried out by people familiar with the victim and complete strangers too. Cyberbullying provides no escape because people share the information until it becomes uncontrollable.

However, the good news is that different social media have defined ways of reporting inappropriate information and images. If you come across such information, you can always share and have the information pulled down.

Cyberbullying has been a cause of suicide among young people. Information on social media becomes public knowledge within minutes of sharing and can be very damaging to a person.

Effects of cyberbullying on teenagers:

The victim feels overwhelmed, and as if they no longer have control over their lives. This feeling comes when so many people are after you with mean messages.

The victim also feels powerless in escaping the situation. The torment follows the victim from school to home and no place id's free from the bullying.

The victim goes through humiliation and feels very exposed. When information is out on the internet, there is no way of getting it back. It remains in circulation till no one finds interest in springing it or focusing attention on it.

Cyberbullying results in the victim losing their self-esteem. Cyberbullies attack the victim with their points of weakness, and this can be very damaging to young people mostly. It causes teenagers to do harmful things that can result in fatality.

In cases where the victim knows the bully, it is only normal to have some sort of revenge by bullying back. This is much worse than just walking away because they both become bullies, and the situation gets worse when none is giving in. It is wise for parents to advise their children going through cyberbullying to just ignore, and not give the bully any attention. If the bully doesn't get the reaction he or she was aiming at from the victim, he'll just stop.

Cyberbullying leads to isolation as the victim finds difficulties in associating with other people. This leads to the victim being lonely and depressed.

The victim also loses interest in activities they once enjoyed and life in general. Bullying leaves the person feeling beaten and unwilling to involve oneself in anything; even normal activities such as schooling and taking a shower.

Feeling ill and stressed – A victim of bullying will always feel stressed and under pressure. These feelings can result in stress-related illnesses such as stomach pains and indigestion, and headaches.

If your child is being bullied, try identifying the source of cyberbullying and put a time to a stop. Take keep attention to the child and if you feel like there is a need for a professional intervention do not hesitate to get one. Let your child know that they should not suffer in silence rather they should have the bully reported to the necessary authority and necessary measures taken into consideration.

Cyberbullying can cause a teenager to drop behind in school, and this may result in poor performance. Depending on the victim's reaction, they may decide to drop out of school. If a parent realizes that their child is disinterested in academics or missing out on classes, it is important to talk to the child and hear them out. They might be suffering in silence.

Drugs and Alcohol

According to research, 8 out of every 10 teenagers in the US take alcohol. This makes alcohol one of the highly abused substance in the united states. The statistics are shocking to every parent. Teenagers take drugs for various reasons:

Some teenagers will go for drugs because they feel left out with the assumption that everyone else is doing it. Others will do it in order to gain g acceptance into certain social groups.

Another reason for engaging in drugs is because someone wants to have fun. The feelings that come with drugs can be said to be relaxing or euphoric. Once a child uses the drugs and gets that feeling, they will want to try it again and, in the end, may end up getting addicted to the drugs.

Others will do drugs out of stress and depression. Taking drugs makes the feeling of stress go way just for the time being. The chances of being addicted are quite high. When the drugs wear off, the person will end up doing them again because they will not be able to deal with reality.

Others will do drugs just out of curiosity. The daring nature of teens causes them to experiment with different drugs just to have a new experience.

How can you tell your child is into drugs?

Drugs can result in drastic changes in a person's life. When a person starts taking drugs, certain aspects of his life will change. Here are some leads to find out if your child is engaging in drugs:

If you find your child in possession of some drugs, there is no other reasonable explanation the child can give without leaving suspicion.

Strange smells like that of bang or marijuana on your child could be a sign he or she is using drugs.

Mood variations in your child that you can't explain could be another sign.

If your child looks stoned all the time with glazed looks, he or she could be already hitched on drugs, and it's time to get the child help.

Drastic drop in academic performance should be questionable to any parent.

If your child is hanging out with a crowd that is known for using drugs all of a sudden, then he might have been initiated into drugs.

An unexplainable change is the social activities the child once used to enjoy being part of, and he or she does not seem interested should raise eyebrows.

If you can't get straight answers to your child's whereabouts, it is good to do more investigations.

If your child is finding difficulties in recalling obvious events, then this is a sign of having been under the influence of drugs.

When your child comes home with some unexplained injuries, then it is good to do your own investigation to establish the causes.

Stealing habits in your child could be another sign. Drugs use is mostly associated with stealing because the person has to sustain the drugs. If your child suddenly starts stealing money and other items that can easily be liquidated, then it is time to get the child help.

Drugs use is related to some health issues. If your child shows any symptoms associated with drug use, then they might be using them.

Weight loss in a child is also something that parents should worry about. Most people who use drugs suffer low appetite, and others don't buy food in order to spare money for drugs.

A child who normally get home early is seen to have shifted to getting home late without any reasonable explanation calls for the parent to check into his or her whereabouts.

How do you handle a child who is taking drugs?

There are certain steps a parent can take when they find out that their child is involved in drugs. If your child is still high on drugs, just let him or her somber up because any conversation you will be having is fertile. Also, let yourself calm down. Otherwise, you will only be shouting and screaming with frustrations and anger which is normal. Thirdly, figure out with the other parent how to handle the situation before you start talking to the child. Both parents need to have a plan of action on how to deal with the problem before you start with the child. You also need to present a united front as you talk so that the child can take the talk seriously.

Let your child understand all the implications associated with the use of drugs. Whatever actions you take, the child should be made to understand that it is for their own good. At this point, you should let your child feel that you love and support his wellbeing. If your child feels that genuine affection, he or she will open up.

Be firm when talking to your child about your plan of action. The parents should let the child know that he or she has to stop taking drugs by all cost, and you as parents will do what it takes to make sure he or she gets help.

Have your child see a doctor or health specialist. Your child will definitely need help. You can talk your child into agreeing to go for rehabilitation willingly; though it would not be easy. But if he or she is not willing, you would have no choice but to force him or her to go for rehabilitation. You could also involve the help of a formal interventionist who is certified to help with the process of getting your child rehabilitated. When deciding on the mode of treatment for your child, the child should be assessed for the underlying causes of the addiction such as depression.

Parental support during the child's treatment and recovery are very important. The parents should be willing to do whatever the doctor recommends in order to have the child fully recovered. This includes caring for the child emotionally and financially and being cooperative in attending all the appointments and giving the child privacy whenever needed.

The parents of a recovering addict should keep all the drugs and alcohol out of the house. The whole family should also abstain from drugs to help the child in the recovery process.

Handling a relapse

Parents need to realize that relapse is common during the recovery process, especially in the first three months. If a relapse occurs, parents should be patient with the child and seek the necessary help. Establishing strict rules for a child in recovery would help to prevent the occurrence of a relapse. However, if your child has gone into a relapse, you will need to consider inpatient treatment services. Parents should also watch out for signs of relapse from their recovering children. The signs are similar to the ones your child showed while he or she was using drugs. A doctor would also advise on drug tests to follow up in monitoring the progress of the recovering addict.

Obesity and Eating Disorders

Desperate weight loss efforts are mostly attributed to incidents of eating disorders. Teenagers are very involved in their body's appearance, and those overweight are subject to bullying. The images presented by the media promoting slim looking appearances as being appealing are major contributors to the desperate pursuit to slimming among the teens. Parents should promote healthy eating habits and exercise to prevent the possibility of their children becoming obese or incurring eating disorders. Teenagers, especially girls, skipping meals in order to reduce weight is quite unhealthy. Teenagers who lose weight abruptly end up suffering from orthostasis, hypotension, bradycardia, and hypothermia. These health conditions can affect even those whose weight is within the recommended range. Gall formation and acute pancreatitis could also result from losing weight too fast.

The obsession with weight loss leads other teens to induce themselves to vomit in an effort to avoid putting on weight. The result of this induced vomiting is electrolyte imbalance. It could also occur when someone goes for long without eating. Amenorrhea is another condition they may occur as a result of the restrictions of the diet. When prolonged, this condition can result in osteoporosis which is a dangerous condition of wearing of bones in the body.

Eating disorders have been associated with teenagers who were once considered to be obese. From the pressures among the peers, the society and some families, the child will forget meals, and whenever they eat, they induce vomiting, or they may go for the dietary pills and excessive exercising without eating properly. In the pursuit of the perfect hourglass figure, the child ends up being treated for eating disorders. Otherwise, the family might be too involved in encouraging the weight loss efforts that the illness is discovered when it's progressed.

Signs to look out for in teens in relation to eating disorders include:

- People are very much interested in exercises.
- Poor nails and loss of hair.
- Dental health problems and cavities.
- Skin problems, such as rashes and scaly skin
- Stomach disorders, such as constipation.
- Insomnia.
- Abruptly changes in weight.
- People always weigh themselves

- Inconsistent eating practices.
- Forgoing meals.
- Inappropriate personal body image.
- Withdrawal from the usual friends' circle.
- People become quite sensitive to personally directed negative comments.

However, parents need to watch their children eating habits. Some of the eating disorders if uncontrolled can be fatal. The good news is that the conditions are curable.

Causes of weight loss and obesity in teenagers

- *Dieting.* This refers to the limitations of the calorie intake aimed at reduction of weight. According to research, dieting has not been effective in weight loss. It has been associated with the risk of both obesity and eating disorders. Most of the people who lose weight through dieting end up gaining the weight back. The teens who engage in dieting to lose weight mostly develop a habit of skipping meals, which eventually turns to eating disorders.

Eating meals as a family has been attributed to reducing the risk of eating disorders and obesity. Family meals encourage healthy eating habits, especially for teenagers and children. They encourage the consumption of more fruits and vegetables, while those who don't often have meals as a family is more prone to taking junk food. It also discourages teenage girls from skipping meals, which when done, extremely leads to eating disorders. Family meals are also an opportunity for parents to take note of the eating habits of their children. They also ensure that children are having balanced diets and consumption of healthy foods.

The weight-related talks parents discuss with reference to themselves or their children have an impact on the eating habits of their children. It all originates from the perception children form on their bodies and the values cultivated in terms of the relation of beauty to weight. Parents should encourage healthy eating habits rather than dieting to cut on weight.

Teasing/mocking teenagers about their weight can be damaging to their eating habits. A child, especially at teenager, will try by all means within their ability to attain an image that's pleasing and attractive. If you keep telling your child that she is too big then she will skip meals if that's what it takes to attain an attractive body shape. On the other hand, telling your child that she is too thin might result in the same child being obese at a later date. Children should feel more comfortable in their bodies, and if a parent feels their child is overweight, they should go for healthy weight loss practices and support their children in going through them. Negative comments about your child will only lead to them acquiring low self-esteem.

Some illnesses might lead to obesity or eating disorders. These illnesses are the likes of neurological disorders and endocrine-related problems. Some medications are also associated with weight gain too.

Genetics also play a role in obesity, among other factors such as poor eating habits. Less active children are also at a higher risk of getting obese.

Problems related to mental health are also a cause for eating disorders and obesity.

Types of Eating Disorders

Binge eating disorder: this involves overeating without the ability to control oneself.

Bulimia nervous: this disorder involves uncontrollable overeating followed by vomiting, which some specialists attribute to feelings of guilt in fear of being overweight. The people with this condition also use diuretics and laxatives. Researchers have also linked bulimia to extreme aerobics. Some of the signs to watch out for include:

- Disruption of the menstrual cycles.
- Excessively exercising
- Use of laxatives and diuretics
- Drugs abuse and alcohol
- Depression
- Disappearing after meals
- Feeling out of control
- Overeating when distressed
- Binge followed by extreme dieting
- Excessive weight worries.

Anorexia nervosa is associated with a person being constantly obsessed with losing weight. People with this condition are always underweight, and they associate their beauty to their weight. This disorder is commonly linked with people with low self-esteem.

Peer Pressure

Peers are people of the same age, sharing some values. Peer pressure is perceived when someone wants to belong to certain groups and ends up conforming with their habits and behaviors to fit in. Peer pressure can affect your child's behavior positively or negatively. From early ages, parents should equipment their children with critical decision-making skills which are very helpful in the choice of friends. Ability to make decisions is also helpful for a child in knowing when the situations demand a firm 'NO' to friends demands. A child with the ability to make independent decisions will not bow to peer pressure easily.

How can you help your child stay off peer pressure?

- Parents should train their children how to say 'No' and mean it. This should come right from home. Wherever your child is unsure of a choice, the parents should teach them to simply admit that they are not sure about it. Children should also be taught not to engage in activities they are not fully decided on. Influence from friends leads to many children in engaging in activities they are not ready to undertake such associated alcohol and premature sex.
- Children should also be raised with information on how to communicate effectively with body language. Teenagers often say no by word of mouth while their nonverbal skills express completely different answers. With these mixed signals, the peers take advantage and pressure the child into engaging in actions they end up regretting about.
- A child with the ability to offer alternative solutions that are more acceptable will not be easily cowed to irresponsible behavior. As a parent, train your child to give alternatives to things they could engage in – things that does not conflict with your own set of morals. A child with these abilities will also be a positive influence

on his or her friends.

- The values a parent trains his children will result in a lot of conflict within the child whenever they try to go against them. It is through these values that a child stays free from negative influence. Reinforcing strong values to your children is very important in maintaining acceptable morals as they grow up.
- Be your children's role model. Your children should be able to learn strong values from you. As you teach your children morals, they should be able to relate those morals with your own actions. Practicing what you preach will also earn you respect from your children, leading them to obey your instructions and teachings.
- There is a common misconception that teens are more influenced by their peers than their own parents, but the reality is no child wants to break the parents' trust. The more parents stop overrating the impact of peers on teens, the easier it is for them to guide their children in living a more rewarding life free from negative peer influence.

The Social Media

Literally, every adolescent is on social media; they live by social media. For this reason, social media has been a major factor in the formation of values, behaviors and attitudes.

Effects of the social media on teens behaviors, values and attitudes:

The social media has been a leading cause of depression and anxiety among teenagers and young people.

Social media anxiety disorder

Social media anxiety disorder is a major mental issue affecting at least 20% of people with social media accounts. This disorder is characterized by:

- Getting anxious and nervous when a person can't access their social media.
- The social media taking up most your waking hours up to 6 hours a day.

- Keeping your phone close all the time in order to check your social media.
- Constantly sharing every aspect of your life on social media.
- Withdrawal symptoms related to the inability to access social media.
- Abandoning important normal life activities involving work, friends, and family for social media.
- Being in a situation where, however much you try to reduce the social media usage, you find difficulties.
- A person might also find themselves being dishonest about the duration he or she spends on social media sites.
- Whenever you are having a conversation, you find yourself being tempted to check your social media.

How to Avoid Social Media Anxiety Disorder

Research suggests that for a child to be able to have a healthy relationship with social media, they need to have an effective communication system at home. Parents have a role to play here by keeping themselves free of their phones and laptops at home. The establishment of strict rules governing the use of phones at home is a way of dealing with addiction to social media. Parents need to ban the use of phones at the dinner table, breakfast, and other occasions when the family needs to be having healthy conversations. Parents should also discourage the carrying of phones to bed by their children because they are attributed to increased insomnia.

Talking to the children about the effects of excessive use of the social media would bring some understanding that might reduce the impact and the resistance that would result from parents banning the use of phones at certain times of the day and night.

Physical Risks Associated with the Use of the Social Media

The social media has been related to some physical health conditions such as lower back and neck pains, and eye problems. Sitting too long while on social media can result in heart-related problems and obesity due to lack of exercise.

Mental Health Problems Resulting from the Use of Social

Media

The use of social media has been associated with:

- Loneliness
- Paranoia
- Impulsive disorder
- Attention deficit hyperactivity disorder ADHD
- Depression

Social media is about sharing, and when it comes to teenagers, most of them will want to feature every integral part of their lives on social media. Teenagers will keep comparing their lives to those of their peers as they appear on social media and feel inferior. These feelings of not living as much as their peers lead to low self-esteem. Others will want to do what they perceive their peers are doing as per their social media posts. The use of drugs and substance abuse has also been promoted by social media. For instance, when a teen sees their friends posting photos in parties and clubs and taking alcohol, such posts attract more comments and likes because they are perceived to be cool.

The social media has also led to most teenagers living fake lives that are misleading to others. Taking photos at exquisite places promotes jealousy among teens who get the feeling that their parents are extremely not doing enough to give them a good life. Parents need to make their teenagers understand that the lives they see people living on social media is all fake just meant to seek attention. They should also discourage their children from getting too much involved in social media.

Parents can use the application to monitor their children's use of social media. This allows for the regulation of the number of time children spend on social media.

It is, however, most important if your child is able to regulate their own use of social media. Parents should have conversations around social media--regarding the type of material they post and how it might affect their future. Currently, employers and admitting panels to colleges are going through social media in order to identify the kind of person they are about to give a job or admit to their institutions. This calls for limited social media life and utmost regulation of posts; keeping in mind that once you make a post, it's no longer private.

Chapter 7: How to Help Youths Find Their Own Path of Faith and Spirituality

Spirituality is a deep connection between someone's spirit/soul with power higher than him or herself. It helps people find their purpose in life. It can be connected to faith in God, art or nature.

Matters of faith and spirituality are personal. The connection a person has whether a child or an adult is so deep for anyone to comprehend even the parents.

However, as parents, we will find it right to initiate our children to our own faith and beliefs. However, assuming the child grows up to a teenager, they may start questioning what they believe in. At this point, the child would have been familiarized with different spiritual beliefs. It will not come as a surprise if your child chooses to change from your faith to another.

What is the purpose of being spiritual?

Being spiritual drives someone's purpose in life. Spirituality defines a certain destiny when all is done. That destiny is not accomplished until the life in this world is done. Without having a purpose, people find no sense in living; especially when encountered with difficulties. People who have no spirituality live on the pleasures of the world which are not able to satisfy their inner needs; they are constantly searching for a purpose, which can only be found in having faith in a greater power.

Spirituality defines a certain set of values that give moral guidance. These values will help your child in relating to other people and forming healthy relationships with everyone in their circle. It also guides their decisions and choices through conscience. One's conscience helps in deterring him or her from doing what goes against their set of values and beliefs.

Spirituality drives a person towards a certain reward, which makes them want to live a morally upright life. When you raise your child in a spiritual environment, you will not have difficulties controlling their behavior. Their behavior will be based on what moral values you grow in them.

People who have faith in a greater being/God don't get easily depressed. If you grow your children in faith, they will always be frenetic about their purpose and strength through connection with their spirituality.

Molding your child's spirituality

- Have conversations around faith. You should bring up conversations around faith with your children from an early age. You can talk to them about your own beliefs and your values based on those beliefs. From an early age, your children will follow your spiritual beliefs though they might change along the way as they grow up, your faith will form their background, and those beliefs will last in them for a very long time. Let your children understand why you believe what you believe and what role faith plays in your life, like giving real-life experiences.
- Let them ask questions. As your child grows in faith, they will ask a lot of questions. The more those questions are answered, the more they keep getting rid of doubts and growing stronger in faith. Give them as many answers as you can. Spiritual questions are difficult to answer because it is not tangible, and most of the things believed in cannot be seen. However, you could enroll them for classes and spiritual groups which can give them more guidance to understand more about faith.
- Have spiritual books and movies. Provide them with spiritual materials that will grow them deeper in faith. You could read books and share what you read. Your child will give you their own views on what they understood. You can offer deep explanations of the same. Watching movies related to faith as a family could help your share in beliefs and values helping your child get insight on right and wrong.
- Don't encourage your child to keep changing their spiritual beliefs constantly. The beliefs articulated in different types of faith can be conflicting, and shifting from one end belief to another could lead to more harm to a young person because it leads to confusion in the young mind.
- Be their role model. Modeling for your child by practicing what you preach will grow their faith in believing what you do with conviction. Whenever your children see you living according to your faith, they will find it easier to believe without doubts.

- Do not coerce your children. Try to explain to your children right from the time they can understand what you believe in. Teach them the values related to your faith and put them into practice as a family. It might not be hard for children below 13 years to follow your faith. However, as they get into their teenage years, they might start questioning your beliefs and however, much obvious they seem to you, they might reject them. If your child doesn't want to follow your beliefs, you can provide them with an option that you find acceptable so that they can choose. However, forcing your beliefs on them will not make them grow in faith. This might lead to them defying once they leave your house and forming a negative attitude towards faith. They might associate faith to a sort of punishment which they can't wait to get rid of.
- Let your child participate in spiritual events. Giving your children opportunities to participate in spiritual events will increase their faith and help them in making friends with similar beliefs, which can be a good influenced on them. It is not debatable that teenagers are very much excited by being part of a group with their peers.

How to Deal with Doubts and Daily Struggles

When it comes to spirituality, sometimes it poses a huge challenge on everyone, not just young people. At times of hardships, it becomes even more difficult to believe, but the intensity of your faith will determine if you get off stronger or you just give it all up and stop believing. For young people or teenagers, you will find seasons of heightened belief and others when they just want to flow with the current. Strengthening your child's faith would help her or him in dealing with doubts and struggles.

Having strong role models in faith, especially parents, would help a teenager in times of spiritual struggles. A child experiencing some uncertainties in faith could also seek help from religious leaders and other leaders in peer groups.

Making your spiritual beliefs a way of life in the family could help keep the children strongly hooked in faith. Family offers an unconditional support system as a unit in guiding one another and even in difficult times.

Having friends who share in your faith could be helpful. Encourage your child to attend religious youth-related functions where they can find friends who would help them grow spiritually. At those trying moments, your child will have a lot of support from these friends.

Reading spiritual materials and watching related information could help a child struggling in faith. It reaffirms a person's spirituality. For instance, through listening or reading other people's testimonies regarding faith could help a person renew their faith.